Write to Launch

Other books by Kylie Dunn

Do Share Inspire: The Year I Changed My Life Through TED Talks

Living With Intent: The 10 Steps to Defining Your Why from My Year of TED

Disclaimer

Since we don't live in an obvious world, here are a few rather obvious facts I thought I should start with.

I have personal experience in self-publishing. I do not have qualifications, certifications or professional experience that might make you think I am a publishing expert. Instead, I am an enthusiastic amateur who is sharing her experiences, learnings and lessons with other like-minded people, who might be crazy enough to start a self-publishing journey of their own.

The content in this book is true and accurate at the time of publication. Given the fast-paced world we live in, that is likely to mean that at least some element of this book is now possibly outdated. Self-publishing is a rapidly changing industry, and I do not plan to validate and update the content in this book every couple of months to ensure it is all still completely accurate. I will update the links to resources on the website, and if something huge occurs in self-publishing I might issue a second edition of this book.

The content is subjective to my experiences and the sources I've used. All care has been taken to cover off this content in an even and considered manner, but it is still slanted to my personal opinions and experience. Like most people, my experiences are limited to some degree, so you need to apply critical thinking as to whether said advice suits your situation. I assume no responsibility for the accuracy of this advice and how it applies to *your* self-publishing journey; just like you assume no responsibility for recommending a restaurant to a friend or setting up your cousin Phil on a blind date with a work colleague.

write to
LAUNCH

A Step-by-Step Guide to Self-Publishing

KYLIE DUNN

dinkylune

First Published in Australia in 2016 by dinkylune –
www.dinkylune.com

Copyright © 2016 by Kylie Dunn

The moral right of the author has been asserted.

National Library of Australia Cataloguing-in-Publication entry:
Dunn, Kylie Louise, 1972- author.
Write to launch : a step-by-step guide to self-publishing / Kylie Dunn.

ISBN: 9780992358358 (paperback)
Self-publishing--Australia--Handbooks, manuals, etc.
Publishers and publishing--Australia--Handbooks, manuals, etc.
070.5930994

Printed and bound in Australia, United States or United Kingdom by IngramSpark, Lightning Source Inc.

CONTENTS

For Derek, who had to endure me learning many of these lessons the hard way, and still supported me doing it again.

Introduction

So you want to write a book? Why? No, seriously. You need to understand why you want to publish a book in the first place. Do you have amazing knowledge or information you want to share with other people? Do you want to grow your audience and your status as an authority? Do you have a desire to see your name on a book cover? Do you want to make a lot of money? That last one is extremely unlikely from the book alone.

I hope that you are doing this because you have an underlying passion to write and share something that is important to you. This could be fiction or non-fiction. Most of my advice in this book is focused on publishing non-fiction, although much of it still applies to publishing fiction too.

If you're reading this, then you're also interested in self-publishing said book. That's great, because the growth of truly independent self-publishing services, ebooks and print-on-demand technology has empowered writers with autonomy from the traditional publishing gatekeepers. This freedom comes with its own potential issues and considerations.

WE LIVE IN A THRILLING TIME, WHERE TRADITIONAL INDUSTRIES ARE CONSTANTLY CHALLENGED; WHERE WE ARE NO LONGER BEHOLDEN TO THE 'EXPERTS' AND GATEKEEPERS

Mainly, self-publishing isn't simply about taking your Word document and turning it into a book. As you will discover here, there are so many other elements to consider. Because self-publishing requires self-managing, self-marketing, self-organising, self-awareness and more self-confidence than many authors possess.

Simply put, just because you *can* publish your own book, it doesn't mean that you should. I am not here to discourage you; the aim of this book is to provide you with the tools to successfully undertake a self-publishing journey. But, I want to make sure you understand exactly what it means to self-publish your book. You are taking on the role of publisher, as well as all of the other functions that a traditional publisher performs – critical analysis, funding, marketing, editing, distribution, promotion, public relations, organisation, administration, legal requirements and design. You will not perform all of these tasks yourself, which means you also need to manage sub-contracting specialists to look after certain activities.

Furthermore, you are not guaranteed any degree of success in this endeavour, no matter how hard you try. Your book might not find an audience, or it might end up in too competitive a market. You can follow one of the dozens of launch 'systems' that are currently popular, and still not manage to gain traction; no one can guarantee that you will.

All of this is not designed to put you off, only to manage your expectations and understanding of what you are about to tackle. Because I can guarantee that if you put in the hard work and follow the steps in this book, you will give your book a great chance of success.

We live in a thrilling time, where traditional industries are constantly challenged; where we are no longer beholden to the 'experts' and gatekeepers. Self-publishing provides you with an incredible opportunity, one that none of our ancestors possessed. And I can tell you from experience – from the experience of someone who always wanted to write books – there is nothing quite like holding a physical copy of a 'real' book that you created and brought into the world.

If you want to write a book; if you are brave enough to tackle all of the tasks and responsibilities mentioned earlier; if you have the courage to give yourself permission to own your publishing journey – then I'd love nothing more than to guide you through the process.

So What's it All About?

The purpose of this book is to lead you through the entire process of writing and launching a book. It started with me capturing the process I took while self-publishing *Do Share Inspire: The Year I Changed My Life Through TED Talks*. It was initially just a project plan of sorts, a list of tasks to complete, taking into account many of the lessons I learned when I was getting things wrong along the way. I've fleshed that content out a lot in this book, including wisdom from my own lessons, and a myriad of other sources that have helped me understand the self-publishing world over the last couple of years.

I should explain that *Do Share Inspire* was not my first self-published book, and this isn't my first guide about self-publishing. In late 2013, I self-published my first ebook, *Living with Intent: The 10 Step Process to Defining Your Why from My Year of TED*. I learned a lot about the technical side of self-publishing, and gathered some of that into a free ebook I gave to subscribers; called *After the Writing: A Short Guide on Navigating the Self-Publishing World*. Some of that content is in this book.

Living with Intent was only an ebook, and there were many publishing decisions I made that I came to realise limited my reach and marketing. When I decided to publish *Do Share Inspire*, that was something altogether different. That book is about 300 pages long, and I wanted to publish it as a paperback, not just an ebook. It was different in many other ways too; ways that have required me to learn a lot more about publishing, and about marketing. I haven't quite nutted out all the marketing elements yet, but I have started getting some traction with publicity; I'll explain more about that as we go along.

In the back of this book, you'll find a list of resources that have contributed to my knowledge and understanding of this process; above my own experience of course. What I'm explaining here is largely common knowledge – in that you can find free resources that will briefly explain the three steps to writing a book, or the launch process that will 'guarantee' you become a bestseller (remember don't be fooled, there is no guarantee).

But what I aim to give you, over and above those free resources, is more of a step-by-step process you can follow, to take the mysticism out of self-publishing, and to stop you from making some of the mistakes I did.

There are resources for you to download on the website – so don't forget to download them now. Visit dinkylune.com/wtlstuff; you'll need the password, which is **Sc@recr0w**.

It might also be helpful for you to use the following graphic as a guidepost for the content in this book. It is a basic outline of the five stages I refer to, although it is not a sequential collection of steps – there is an overview in your downloads that provides a better indication of sequence.

SELF-PUBLISH IN FIVE STAGES

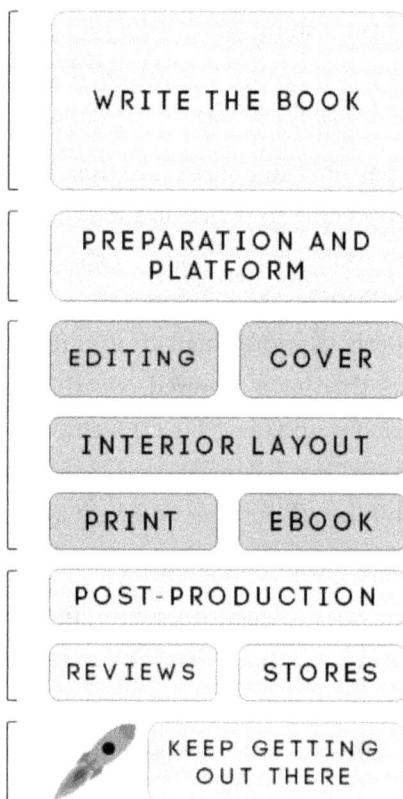

WRITE THE BOOK

PREPARATION AND PLATFORM

EDITING COVER

INTERIOR LAYOUT

PRINT EBOOK

POST-PRODUCTION

REVIEWS STORES

KEEP GETTING OUT THERE

For now, let's get started with writing the book.

Stage One – Writing the Book

OUTLINING YOUR CONTENT

The first step is to work out what you want to write about and structure the content. If you are reading this you may already have an idea, structure and content for your book. If you have already written your book, skip to Reference Material.

I'm not going to get into idea generation with you. If you don't know what you want to write a book about, then you need to think about whether you really want to publish a book.

When you have your idea, you need to create a structure to start writing. One of the biggest issues people have when they start writing anything is that they fail to plan. You should never start writing without having a clear idea of the following:

- The purpose of your book – e.g. authority, money, audience, sharing, lead generation.

- Your ideal audience – remember you can't write for everyone, or your message will be too broad and thus ineffective.

- What you want your audience to do – this could be the message you want them to walk away with, or the action you want them to take.

- The content you need to include to inform, influence or convince the audience to do what you want them to do.

Let's use *Do Share Inspire* as an example:

- The purpose of this book was two-fold. Mainly I was publishing it to share my story and knowledge with others. It was also to help build my audience.

- My ideal audience is me or, more precisely, me pre-My Year of TED. So, women in their late 30s to early 40s who want to sort out their lives and start pursuing activities that will help them be more fulfilled. I have a much more detailed description of this that I work to.

- I want my audience to do two things. First, I want them to understand that they can give themselves permission to make the changes they want to make to their lives. Second, I hope that they will be inspired to take on at least one of the activities for themselves, and start making those changes.

- The content for this book was easy, since I'd already written the blog. I did have to structure an introduction and conclusion of sorts though, so I needed to think about setting it up and wrapping it up.

Do you want another one? The book that you are reading now went like this:

- Purpose: again this is mainly sharing, but there is part of this that is building authority as well. You see, helping other people through the self-publishing process in an inexpensive way lends itself heavily to my Why. What is a Why? Simon Sinek explains this well in his incredibly popular TED Talk, but it is the reason behind What we do and How we do it.

- My ideal audience is someone who is serious about self-publishing a book, but isn't sure how it works or where to start. Yes, this is a lot broader than *Do Share Inspire*, but again I'm not about convincing you to write a book.

- I want my audience to get off their butts and follow the process to successfully self-publish their first book.

- The content for this started with the list I created of tasks when I was self-publishing. I combined this with advice about writing from the courses I facilitate; advice and tips from a myriad of sources; and my previous self-publishing book. All of these provided an outline of tasks, which I chunked into different stages, then fleshed out the content within. I will mention that I mindmapped this – I work better with visual notetaking, and I find that mindmaps are more flexible than lists.

A mindmap is a visual representation of ideas. It starts with the central idea, let's say 'self-publishing'. You create sub-categories or subjects related to that original idea, either as words, symbols or drawings. Lower level topics are then included, grouped under the sub-categories. Connectors are used to join the concepts to the right subject; sometimes a concept might connect to multiple subjects. Below is a tidied up mindmap for this book.

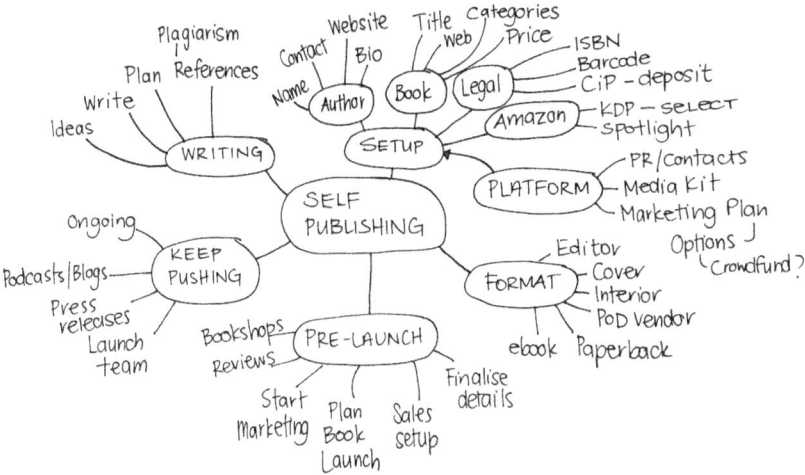

Figure 1: Mindmap of content for self-publishing book

Action

I would encourage you to stop now and work this out for your book. Even if it is just the broad headings for your content and the journey you plan to take your reader on – yes, even if it is a non-fiction book your job is to take them on a journey.

GROUP CONTENT INTO CHAPTERS

As you are mindmapping or listing, you should be grouping the content into logical chunks, which will likely become your chapters. One of the biggest problems when we're writing on a topic we are expert in, or incredibly familiar with, is we forget to include the simple details. You know how this works. There is knowledge that is second nature to you, so obvious that you fail to mention it – but someone reading your book might be a complete beginner.

Being familiar enough with a topic that you are writing a book about it may mean you are too close to it to truly understand what you need to include in the book. Maybe details and knowledge have become so ingrained you don't even think about explaining them. Or maybe you've never had to explain this topic to someone before, and you don't know where to start.

Some prompts to start this process would be:

- When you are performing a task, what are the steps you take? You might get down in the weeds, but you can work up from there.

- If you had to explain this to a five-year-old, how would you do that? This is great for developing a high level, simple starting point.

- What are the journalistic six for the topic? Mindmap using Who, What, When, Where, Why and How headings for the topic/process/story.

- Find someone in your life who knows nothing about the topic and have an instructional conversation with them. Write down their questions and the topics you cover. Work out what you have to explain to them in a half hour or hour long conversation so they can get the point of your book.

Group and regroup again until you have identified a structure for sorting your information and knowledge. Then, and this is extremely important, be willing to restructure it when you start writing and realise it needs to change. You are unlikely to get this perfect in the structuring stage, but if you try to write without going through this process you will end up reworking it a lot more – and you'll end up with more writer's block and procrastination as well, trust me.

WRITE CONTENT

START WRITING, REMEMBERING THAT YOUR WRITING BRAIN AND EDITING BRAIN ARE TWO DIFFERENT FUNCTIONS

This is not a book about how to write, but I couldn't publish this book without a few tips on writing. Some of these are encapsulated in the advice above, but repetition improves retention:

1. Know the context, purpose and audience for your content before you start.

2. Outline your content and work out the basic structure for it.

3. Conduct any research required, ensuring you keep track of all of your sources.

4. Ensure you incorporate factual information and stories. Remember that people don't connect with facts and figures; the stories that you share will connect with your readers, then they will look for the factual information to support their feelings and opinions.

5. Start writing, remembering that your writing brain and editing brain are two different functions. Give yourself the creative freedom to write your first draft without editing as you go – the content will flow much better, you will avoid writer's block, and you are the only one who will see that draft anyway.

6. Rewrite your content until you are happy with it, before you give it to an editor. However, know it will never be perfect and you have to let it go – at least three drafts, no more than six.

7. Keep your language plain, positive, simple and connected with the audience. Don't shift to writing in a third person, passive, disconnected way – own what you are saying and keep it in active tense. Avoid clichés; consider whether you can use metaphors to explain subjects; remove all of the irrelevant words and jargon; be aware of your 'go to' phrases, and either replace or remove them.

8. Start considering the format for the content, particularly whether you are going to include graphs, images, or other visual indicators that need to be developed with the content.

Speaking your book

Okay, I can't write this and not talk about the current wisdom of 'speaking your book' and having someone transcribe it. I will admit that this advice rankles with me, because you should be WRITING your book; we don't call authors 'talkers'. Having said that, I do understand the advice, but I think it has to come with some hefty caveats:

- You still have to have all of the pre-work done – just because you aren't sitting down to type, it doesn't mean that all of the steps before this are irrelevant. If anything, it is more important for you to have a fully fleshed out structure before starting, because it is not as easy for you to refer back to what you said previously.

- The process of speaking your book will only give you the rough first draft – do not even contemplate the thought that the transcribed text will be good enough to publish! It will be a first draft that you should take through at least a second draft stage, before you give it to an editor. I've seen what happens when this is not done, and it's generally a painful and confusing read.

By all means, if you are not a great typist, record yourself speaking the content of your book and pay someone to transcribe it – just remember it is a first draft, and there is still a long way to go before it is something you should be publishing.

REFERENCE MATERIAL

Let's talk a little about plagiarism

Maybe you aren't familiar with the laws that exist around using other people's content or ideas as your own. Most of us get a brief introduction to it at school and university. Sadly, with the advent of Creative Commons and the ease with which we can take other people's content and 're-purpose' it for our own ends on the internet, the old rules seem to have been forgotten.

The Oxford dictionary definition of plagiarism is 'the practice of taking someone else's work or ideas and passing them off as one's own'. And it is just as applicable in the online space as it is in printed media, though far more difficult to police. In simple terms, if I take someone's article or content and reproduce it with no attribution to the original author – that is plagiarism. Even if I am only copying a paragraph of content, I should still reference the source; it was their work, not mine.

What about if I am using their concept/idea as the basis for creating an entirely new piece of content (not just regurgitating it)? As long as you have not copied their work, and you have significantly contributed something new to the idea, then technically it is not plagiarism. However, it is still polite to give credit where credit is due. I know this can become difficult, if you are developing something that might have been inspired by five different people over a long period of time. So follow this rule: if you know where it came from, credit them.

This is a problem I am dealing with writing this book. I started reading blogs and books, and watching webinars on self-publishing about four years ago. Over that time, I've taken a snippet from here, a piece of information from there, and a tip from I can't even remember where. As a result, I can't definitely tell you where some of these ideas come from, or what influenced me. That's why, at the end of this book there is a long list of sources and resources that have likely influenced my self-publishing journey, and the content in this book. That is the best I can do without revisiting all of the content, and likely attributing certain pieces of advice to at least 10 sources. Where I know it is one person's influence alone, I will ensure I include that reference.

Stealing and copyright infringement

This is akin to plagiarism, but let's call a spade a spade here. Many people produce amazing free content these days; blog posts, articles or freebies for subscribing to the website. It is impossible for anyone to monitor if this content is being used somewhere else. There is an argument that taking and sharing this content is not damaging, because it's not like you are taking away their content – this is akin to the 'video/music piracy is not stealing' argument, but far worse.

In reality, you are depriving the creator of an audience, and possibly sales – here's why:

- I get a free report for signing up to EFG website. I decide to provide it to my readers, or paying clients. I am depriving the creators behind EFG website with subscribers to their website – subscribers who could turn into paying customers.

- I've purchased an online course from XYZ Inc. and I liked the workbook so much I've decided to rebadge it and provide it to my paying customers as part of my own service. This is clearly stealing, since I am passing their content off as my own AND I am charging other people for the material – clearly depriving the creator of paying customers.

If this work is protected by Copyright, then you are likely to be breaking the law if you reproduce, distribute, display or make a derivative product without getting permission.

Re-purposing, a little bit of both

This is the one I have the most trouble with, because many people use it as an excusable means for plagiarising or stealing content. Re-purposing is defined as 'adapt for use in a different purpose'. Let's say I wrote this blog post about plagiarism, copyright and theft (because that is exactly what this section was). About nine months later I decide to write a book about self-publishing and want to include a section on the need to reference material. So, I decide to re-purpose the blog post into this new content. That is how re-purposing works, taking something that **I** created and adapting it for a different audience or purpose – not taking something that someone else created, making minor changes and calling it my own!

Re-purposing is often used as shorthand for plagiarism and stealing. There is a modern definition of the term, particularly online, that seems to be 'taking someone else's content, slapping your logo on it and promoting it as your own'. Nothing could be further from the truth. Taking someone else's content, without their knowledge or permission; rebadging it, without any attribution or credit given to the source; and then passing it off as your own brilliant creation is fraud – it's theft, it's lazy and it's wrong.

A brief note on Creative Commons licenses

There is a lot of content created under Creative Commons (CC) licenses, but there are a variety of CC license conditions – it is not a free-for-all. There are six license options under CC, and the base license still requires you to give the creator credit:

- Attribution (BY)
- Attribution-ShareAlike (BY-SA)
- Attribution-NoDerivs (BY-ND)
- Attribution-NonCommercial (BY-NC)
- Attribution-NonCommercial-ShareAlike (BY-NC-SA)
- Attribution-NonCommercial-NoDerivs (BY-NC-ND)

There is more in the blog post about how you police people copying your material (hint, it is extremely difficult). You can read the whole post at dinkylune.com – there is a link on your resource page.

It is vital that you include references to any material that came from other people. I will admit that this can become problematic, especially if this is an area you've worked in for years, or there are so many resources that you have used that have the same advice (like this book). So start with quotes, activities, statistics and images – most of these will have come from another source, so make sure they are all appropriately referenced. Even if you have significantly redeveloped an activity that was based on someone else's work, give them credit for the original idea that you reworked; credit where credit is due.

At this point you also need to decide whether you are going to include footnotes or endnotes. I would recommend endnotes if you are planning on publishing an ebook. They are a flowing structure without clear pages; endnotes work better for that format.

Seek license authority to use copyright materials

Remember, if you plan on using copyrighted material or information in your book, you need to seek approval for that. Most content creators would be happy to allow you to use their work, as long as it is properly credited and acknowledged – and you're adding your own knowledge and value to it. Get in contact with them and ask. If they say no, respect that and find another way to explain or illustrate your point without it.

DRAFT ACKNOWLEDGEMENTS

This is that page in a book where you get to thank and acknowledge the support and contributions of others to your book. You could write this later in the process, the only reason I suggest doing it now is that you can have your editor review that content at the same time as your book. If you do it later, you might need to re-engage your editor for a page or two of content – yep, this point comes from experience.

It's important for you to include this because our knowledge is the sum of other people in our lives. You might have developed a process or come up with an idea, but you didn't do that in a vacuum. You did that by joining together ideas and concepts from others, or by working with other people to understand what you need your process to do. Your book is not all about you, even if it's a biography or memoir.

Stage Two – Creating Your Platform

This is the most detailed stage of the process. It includes tasks you can start during Stage One, and other tasks that will be finalised in Stage Four. This section is about:

- Setting yourself up as an author.

- Finalising your book details.

- Legal requirements of publishing a book.

- Setting up your Amazon platform.

- Developing the strategy to market and promote your book.

Basically, it is about how you create a platform for yourself as an author, and the book(s) you publish – a platform to attract your audience and allow you to successfully market your book.

Below is a simple outline of these tasks, some things to consider, and tips that might help.

BECOMING AN AUTHOR

This is not about acquiring a tweed jacket and glasses, it's about setting up your 'author platform'. This is more than simply having a website to sell your book, it's about creating a place for your audience to find you and engage with you. This section includes the key elements.

Finalise Author Name and Contact Info

Most people will publish the book under their own name, but you might want to consider the actual name you use. If you have quite a common name, will you use your middle initial to distinguish yourself? If your name is Michael, but everyone knows you as Mick, which do you publish under? If writing fiction, do you want to use a pen name?

You also need to consider the contact details that you will include on websites, newsletters, press releases and the like. If you have a business address, that makes it easier; if you work from home you might want to consider getting a PO Box, rather than using your home address.

Will you set up an author email address? Or do you create an email address for the book? You definitely want an email address that is separate to your personal email, so important media, reader or publisher information doesn't get caught up in your day-to-day communications. We're going to discuss buying a domain name and setting up a website; most providers will give you a number of email addresses when you do this, so consider an info@ or media@ email address for that domain.

Create Your Author Bio

You will need an author biography for your book, websites and catalogue entries – the sooner you do this, the better. Your author bio can take a multitude of formats or tones, depending on your book and what you want to share. Will it be very personal, so people can connect to you? Is it about your qualifications and career experience, to create authority? Will it be comedic or serious?

It should only be about 150 words long, but you might need a little more backstory, depending on who you are. My author bio is probably a little too long; I think I need to change it to be pithier. My advice on this is go to a bookshop and look at books in your genre – check out the author bios and get an idea of the common structure and content.

Buy the URL of Your Name (and Book Title)

This is not essential, depending on what you intend your book to be. For example, if you're publishing a book essentially as a business card, you might not worry too much about having the domains of your name or the book title. For most of us though, having a website with our name, or the book title, is a vital piece of the puzzle.

If you've never purchased a domain name before, or set up a website, there are many services and people online who can help you – I'm not going to get into it here.

You can consider purchasing multiple domains, if they are available. By this I mean, I have kyliedunn.com and kyliedunn.com.au; having .com is still important, but since I'm Australian I wanted the .au as well. Please don't go crazy though – you'll be offered every possible domain, but you don't need them.

If you can't get your name, get a little clever, but not too clever. Can you abbreviate your name? Add a middle initial? First initial and surname only? Or something like *myname*author? For example, my brother has matthewdunnart.com – since matthewdunn.com was taken. Like I said, get clever, but not so clever people can't find you.

Please don't get the book title domain, unless it is something quite unique. I purchased doshareinspire.com, but I didn't even consider purchasing Living with Intent. I guess what I'm saying is, don't go overboard and purchase a whole heap of domains that nobody is ever likely to go to. They might seem 'cheap', but they do add up over time.

Set Up Your Author Website

Once you have the domain(s), you need to setup an author website. Again, if you don't require an online presence for your book, then feel free to skip this part.

Your author website is there to serve a couple of purposes:

- It tells people more about you, and gives them a way of contacting you.

- It tells people more about the book and where they can buy it – that might even be by purchasing it from your website.

- It gives people updates about future books, book signings (or other events), links to interviews or other relevant information.

- It can be a place where you blog about content related to the book – but this is not essential! Please don't start a blog if you have nothing consistent to say. You don't have to blog weekly, but you should at least be communicating something of interest and value once a month if you are going to blog.

- It is where readers, or potential readers, can sign up to your email newsletter – this one is vital!

YOUR ABILITY TO REACH YOUR AUDIENCE IS ALWAYS LIMITED AND DISTRACTED BY THE PLATFORM YOU USE

Why the email newsletter?

I'm going to talk about social media next, but one of the most important marketing tools that you will have is an email newsletter. You might have thousands of followers on Facebook, Twitter, Instagram, Snapchat – whatever social media platform you like – but your ability to reach them is always limited and distracted by the platform you use.

An email newsletter is in a different space, and they will always see it – unlike social media platforms diminishing the organic reach of posts. Yes, just because it makes it to their email it doesn't mean they will read it, but you have a far greater opportunity they will over the tweet or post that joined hundreds of others in their feed. Also, what if the social media platform shuts down? They aren't your contacts after all, they are part of a third-party service you're using.

A couple of important things I will say about setting up and running your email newsletter:

- Use a service like Mailchimp – I've used them for a few years now, and have only recently started paying for the service, and that was because I wanted some additional functionality. They ensure you meet all the government requirements against SPAM and other related legislation around the world.

- Offer them something of value – this is often called a lead magnet, but it's something you give them for free, for becoming part of your community. I'm sure you've all signed up for free ebooks, a webinar, or something similar, so you know what I mean. *If you're not sure, sign up to my newsletter and see what I give away (ebooks, posters, templates) – kyliedunn.com/signup.*

- Make the newsletter interesting, valuable and non-spammy – don't email too often, and try to keep it consistent (I've failed at this in the past). Don't just make the emails 'buy my stuff'; that's not what they're about. They're about letting the readers behind the scenes of the chocolate factory; or providing valuable content, tips and advice that you don't provide elsewhere. Make it something they want to read, so when your book (or next book) comes out, they are happy for you to have a sales conversation with them – maybe they'll even be keen for it! Oh, and talk about other people too.

Remember, these people are your tribe; they are an essential part of your 'author platform'. Social media followers are a small component of that as well, but the email subscribers are so much more important.

Note: if part of your goal is to be traditionally published, then you need to have a very healthy author platform to get a publishing contract. So don't underestimate the importance of growing your email list.

Set up Social Media Accounts

You might already have social media accounts on some platforms, but you should consider setting up non-personal accounts to publicise your book. I will say that I didn't do this – while I have a My Year of TED page on Facebook, I did not create a whole suite of 'author' accounts. This is largely because I didn't use social media very much for personal interactions before I started doing My Year of TED – the only reason I really started using Facebook was as part of the platform building for that project.

However, if you have a social media account that is connected to all your friends and family, with private and personal content – create something separate to that. Some basic tips for social media are:

- Do not go for every platform, you will be spreading yourself too thin.

- Pick one or two that you know, preferably platforms where you know your audience lives. For example, if 40- to 55-year-old women are your demographic, then Snapchat is unlikely to be the best platform; try Pinterest or Facebook instead.

- Try to get the same username for each of the platforms you have chosen – I am dinkylune on all social media, it's a name I've used for many years (it's an anagram of my name, in case you're wondering) and since kyliedunn was gone on Twitter, I decided to use dinkylune for everything.

- Don't wait until the book launch to start talking about the book; you can start generating buzz beforehand, keeping the points below in mind.

I'll cover these two things a little more in the marketing plan, but as a reminder:

- Follow the 80/20 rule – 80% of your posts should be about other people, relevant topics to your subject, interesting quotes/tips/tools/research, updates that are not trying to sell the book. Only 20% should be focused on selling the book, but do it in a clever way if you can.

- Consider using a service like Hootsuite to help you manage and schedule posts – this is particularly relevant when you are launching the book and want to pre-plan messages and content.

FINALISING THE BOOK DETAILS

Book Title and Subtitle

You thought writing the book was difficult – welcome to the world of titling it! You might be lucky, there might be a title that leaps out at you; that hasn't been used before; that encapsulates your message – but that isn't the case for most people. Titling *Do Share Inspire* was a painful process that caused sleepless nights and angst. This was largely my own fault, because I felt the need to reference My Year of TED in the subtitle – if you remember the published title, that is not in it. Once I set myself free from that limitation, it made the process a lot easier.

I'm yet to find something that will help you title your book, but this is how I tend to do it.

- In 50 words or less, what is your book about?

- Search Amazon for books on this topic – this will help you see the most common title words, and maybe some titles to avoid. I was recently introduced to a tool called KindleSpy that can help with some of the Amazon research (thanks Nick Stephenson).

- If you were looking for advice on the topic, what sort of words would you use to search Google?

- Stream of consciousness – write out words or phrases that you think align to the book or the message.

Note: you cannot copyright a book title, so there is nothing to stop you using the same book title as someone else – my book Living with Intent is an example of this; another book of the same title was published 18 months after mine, and another one published a couple of months ago. I recommend that you try to make it different though, and not just with the subtitle.

With all of these completed, start pulling titles together; remember that clarity is better than making it 'clever'. You want to get it down to three or four at most before you start asking others about it, unless you come up with an absolute winner. This is key though: you want to ask others for input or comment on your title; what is absolutely clear and clever in your eyes might make no sense to others.

Asking others about your book title serves another purpose: it gets them involved with the book and makes them feel like part of the process. This helps you create some buzz about the book, and also gets them invested in the project – you should do this with your cover as well, but we'll get to that.

Write the Book Sales Page

You have the author website; now you need a specific sales page for the book itself. Of course, you can only do all of this once you have the title and book cover sorted out. You can blog about the progress without these things, indeed asking your readership for help with the title and book cover is recommended, but wait until the decisions are made before you set up a sales page.

I'll start this by saying that I generally dislike long-form sales pages; that is a sales page that has a lot of content on it designed to persuade you to buy whatever it is they're selling. Since you are selling a book, which is a low price, this page doesn't need to be as detailed as sales pages for more expensive items. But it's still important for it to contain elements that will help explain why potential readers should buy your book, and what they will get from reading it.

Note: if you purchased this book after visiting my website, you have some idea of the sort of sales page I'm talking about. If not, visit dinkylune.com/writetolaunch, or the Do Share Inspire *page kyliedunn.com/doshareinspire.*

Below are the elements of content required for sales copy of something like a book; and they should generally appear in this order too. This is a mix of multiple sources, but was mainly learned through courses by Ramit Sethi and Ray Edwards. For fiction, your aim is to entice the reader with the story itself, so it is slightly different to the structure below; I've included a few tips for you as well.

- THEIR SITUATION – particularly for non-fiction, what is their current situation and what is the problem you are trying to resolve for them. This is often referred to as their pain point, and you need to tell them how you'll help them solve it. It can work a little for fiction, if you set it up for the story taking them to somewhere wonderful/exciting etc.

- FUTURE PACING – what life will be like after reading your book, compared to if they don't buy. For fiction authors, this could be enticing them with what they will miss, more like your story hook.

- SCARCITY – limited time, limited number, special offer – ACT TODAY! Only include this if there is actual scarcity. Never lie to your audience about a 'limited' anything if it isn't true – don't lie about anything to do with your sales copy.

- STORIES – your personal story on how you became an expert in this, so they can see that you know the topic, and what they're going through. For fiction, this is not essential but could be the authors or books you loved that inspired this; and how important reading has been in your life. You need to build trust through this story; where appropriate, be vulnerable and discuss failures as well as successes.

- SOCIAL PROOF – this is where you prove why you are the person writing this book (non-fiction) or any other credibility you might have as a writer. Include testimonials and some book reviews, and links through to more on Amazon, Goodreads etc. Also, being featured in the media or other websites; blog posts you've written; writing awards or other accolades you have received. This is also where you will mention 'bestseller' numerous times, once you reach that point.

- CONTENT – you need to tell them what they will actually get in the book. You can include your table of contents, a preview of the first chapter, or simply dot-point what they will discover from your book. With fiction, you could also include a sample chapter, although remember to end that sample with a hook, so they need to know what happens next.

Again, go and check out 'like' sales pages online to get a better idea of how this works. Please do not copy other people, and definitely never copy their content – remember plagiarism applies to online content too!

Also, consider recording a brief video introducing yourself and sharing what you hope readers will get from your book. It's another way to connect and increase that trustworthiness. It doesn't have to be professionally filmed, but make sure the tone and presentation match the book.

Set Price on Your Print and eBook Versions

At this stage, you should have a fairly good idea of the word count for your book, but you are unlikely to know the actual page count until the interior is finished in Stage Three. Once you know that, you can work out how much it is going to cost to have your book printed through a print-on-demand (POD) service, I explain print options in detail in

Stage Three. Remember, you can always go somewhere and have 1,000+ copies printed instead of using POD, but there are many reasons why this is a much riskier and more difficult venture for a first time self-publisher.

I'm going to discuss pricing for physical and electronic books separately, for some very obvious reasons, but there are two points to remember:

- You have put time into creating something of value to others and you need to remember that worth when you consider its price.

- You may never recoup all of the costs, particularly the time you put into it, from book sales alone – so do not price it based on the time taken to create it.

Pricing your physical book

You need to understand what it will cost to print your book before you can make an educated guess on pricing it. At this stage, you might have no idea about the dimensions and page count for your book. If that is the case, it is best to wait for the Interior Content task to be completed before you finalise any prices. Actually, at this point I will remind you that some of these steps can occur consecutively – you should not be thinking that you will complete all of the Stage Two tasks before you start Stage Three; see the project overview template for more details.

There are a couple of tips I will give you for pricing your book:

- You will need to give bookshops (including online ones) a 40–50% discount from the retail price – so you need to give yourself some sort of profit margin.

- Go to a bookshop and look at 'like' books – books on similar topics, with similar page lengths and similar dimensions.

- Don't price it above the average from your research – if you want to make money, the process of selling your book is not the way to do it.

- Don't price yourself too far below the average from your research – book buyers are used to paying a certain price for books, so don't penalise yourself.

- Consider the 'retail' price, and what you will sell it for if people buy directly from you – charge less if they buy it from you, because you don't have to share the profit.

Pricing your ebook

The process of pricing a physical book is simple compared with ebooks. There is a cost associated with producing a physical book, people get that; but there is a perception that ebooks should be cheap because, well quite frankly because self-publishers created that perception by making them cheap! We'll get into free copies and reduced prices later, for now here are some things to consider when pricing your ebook:

- The online store will take a small percentage – again make sure you know what this is and price accordingly. Noting that the price really should be the same for an ebook, regardless if it is on Kindle, Barnes and Noble, Apple's iBookstore etc.

- Research like books in your category – again take note of the page length as a differentiator, and see if the book is self-published or done by a publishing house, as this can greatly vary the price.

- You have a lot more room to play, since there are no 'production' costs, but still consider the average price and work around that – people often consider price to be an indicator of worth or value; make it too low and they may be turned off.

Remember that you can always adjust the price, but before you do reduce it, work out whether that is the reason you are having problems selling it first.

Choose Publication Categories – Topic and Sales

Onto a nice simple topic: what is your book about? What category does it best fit into? If people are searching or browsing for a book through categories, which one are they likely to look for? If only it were that easy, but you should have guessed by now there is always more to it.

Simply put, you're going to have to do some research, and Amazon is the best place to do this. You want to find an appropriate category – do not put your book in a completely inappropriate category – but you want to pick a sub-category that you have an outside chance of reaching bestseller status in.

For example, when I was picking categories for *Do Share Inspire* I set about researching 'like' books, and the Amazon categories. I looked at Self-Help – Personal Transformation, because that is probably the most applicable category. At the time I was researching it, Brené Brown and Elizabeth Gilbert held the top spots. There is no way I am ever beating those women in book sales, so I kept looking for other relevant topics. I 'settled', as it were, on Social Philosophy as the category I might be able to top, and Self-Help – Success for a relevant one I might have a chance in.

Remember, you get to pick two categories. Choose honestly and accurately, but you can get a little creative in the process as well.

LEGAL REQUIREMENTS

I'm not going to discuss setting yourself up as a business, contract requirements, or a range of other legal issues here. This is about the legal requirement to register and lodge your book in an appropriate way, within your country.

Not every 'book' will meet these requirements, for example, colouring books are highly unlikely to comply with legal deposit requirements. You will need to check with your national library about what they expect of you as a self-publisher, but the requirements below are fairly standard in Australia, New Zealand, United Kingdom, United States, Canada and similar countries.

Get Your ISBNs

When you publish a book you need an International Standard Book Number (ISBN). This is a unique number that allows people to find your book in a catalogue – you cannot be in a library or physical shop without one. You also can't have an ePub ebook without an ISBN, which needs to be different to your physical book ISBN. You don't need an ISBN for Kindle, because Amazon gives them a different unique code – an Amazon Standard Identification Number (ASIN).

So, if you only plan on publishing a Kindle ebook, you can ignore this section and move on. For everyone else, you need to get an ISBN in your country, and the rules for ISBNs are different, depending on the country in which you are publishing the book. I'm not going to explain it for everyone, because there's Google and you can do some of your own research – you want to self-publish a book don't you?

- In Australia, and the United States, you need to purchase ISBNs from Bowker, or Thorpe-Bowker in Australia. For Australia, the website to do this is myidentifiers.com.au; US is bowker.com.

- In Canada and New Zealand, it's free to get an ISBN allocation. For New Zealand it apparently only takes about three days: natlib.govt.nz. If you're Canadian allow two weeks for processing: bac-lac.gc.ca.

- For the UK, Neilsen manages the allocation of ISBNs. There is also a charge for the codes, and allow at least two weeks, or pay extra to have it processed quickly: isbn.nielsenbook.co.uk.

It is important that you understand and follow the entire process for getting an ISBN, and updating all of the details of your book. I'm not sure how this is done everywhere else; in Australia you get a login to manage your ISBNs, and you update all of the details directly into that database. It's important for you to make sure these details are correct, because this is a legal registration of your book.

Also important is the fact that you need to have an ISBN for each format of the book – so a different ISBN for a paperback and ePub. This often means you will need to purchase or acquire more than one ISBN. For Australia and the US, they are sold individually or in blocks of 10 – my advice is to get a block of 10 if you're thinking you'll publish more than one book. Again, you do not need ISBNs for Kindle books.

Should I use the ISBN provided by the vendor? Some vendors include the provision of an ISBN as part of their service; you do pay for it though. You should know that when you use their ISBN, the book is registered to them as the publisher, which usually means you can't get copies printed elsewhere. Yes, you can still acquire your own ISBN and have other copies printed, but their ISBN ties you to them. Just something to think about.

Get a Barcode for Your ISBN

The ISBN providers will also provide you with barcodes for your physical book – at a price of course. Again, if you plan on selling your book through bookshops, you will need a barcode; you do not require a barcode for an ebook, of course, so don't be conned into purchasing them. There are other ways to get a barcode – you do not have to purchase them from the providers, and those other methods can be a lot more cost effective.

Note: it might be possible to get a free barcode through your POD vendor. For example, if you use IngramSpark, you will use the Cover Template Generator to get the cover template (with barcode) emailed to you before you start the design process – free! Other vendors may do this too, so check before you buy them.

Library Lodgements and Copyright

At this point you should also look at the legal lodgement requirements that might exist in your country for published books. Many countries have a Cataloguing-in-Publication (CiP) program run through their national library. If you are publishing an eligible book, you need to apply for a CiP entry prior to the release of your book. Once this has been processed, you will be provided with the CiP imprint for inclusion in your book. You will also be required to lodge a legal deposit copy once it has been published.

This is my CiP imprint for *Write to Launch:*

National Library of Australia Cataloguing-in-Publication entry:
Dunn, Kylie Louise, 1972- author.
Write to launch : a step-by-step guide to self-publishing / Kylie Dunn.
ISBN: 9780992358358 (paperback)
Self-publishing--Australia--Handbooks, manuals, etc.
Publishers and publishing--Australia--Handbooks, manuals, etc.
070.5930994

Australians are also required to submit a copy of any Australian published book as a legal deposit to their State Library – look up legal deposit on your State Library's website to find out all the required information. If you failed to do a CiP application prior to the publication of your book, then the legal deposit process will create an entry in the national library catalogue anyway.

Look into how this works within your own country, to ensure you meet your legal obligations and copyright requirements for your country. In Australia, our copyright law basically says that as soon as the work is published we own the copyright for it – there are no further steps in the process. In other countries, you may be required to register the copyright for your work, and meeting the legal requirements of your national library is likely to be a part of that.

Please check with your national library before you pay a third-party to do any of this for you; it is likely to be easier than you think, and probably free.

Are you a 'non-resident alien' to the US?

While I'm not going into the taxation and business aspects of selling your book, there is one thing that I think I should mention – since it is likely you will sell your book through at least one US based store.

Most of the sites I have mentioned are businesses located in the United States, which is not surprising. This means that for people who already have a US social security number or tax identification number the process is a lot simpler than for the rest of us. I love this term, a non-resident alien, by the way – definitely a 'not one of us' phrase.

If you are like me, a citizen of another country living outside the US, and have never done this sort of thing before, you can apply to the IRS for an Individual Taxpayer Identification Number (ITIN) and get foreign status for US Tax Withholding from these businesses. But you should know that you are not required to have an ITIN to apply for foreign status – so unless you have another compelling reason, avoid the W–7 process.

Let me start by saying that the IRS is like every other government department that I have ever dealt with throughout the world – with the 'why make it easy when you can confuse the crap out of everyone' ethos. You will need to submit a W–8BEN (the foreign status form) to each of the organisations you are publishing with. This means, you will need to work out which treaty code to use. In the next section, I mention how great Amazon's online form is for navigating this paperwork – so my advice is, **do that one first** and it will help you with the manual forms for the others.

It's annoying to have to do this, but it is part of using US businesses in your revenue generation process. Of course if you are happy for the US Government to keep 30% of your revenue then feel free not to – for us Australians they still keep 5% anyway; it might be more depending on where you live.

Note: there are tax implications in other countries as well, but I have not had to deal with them yet – there may be an update to this at some stage.

SELLING ON AMAZON

Since Amazon is the largest online retailer of books and ebooks, it makes sense that you need to think about how you will use them to sell your book. I'm not going to discuss how you set yourself up as a vendor to sell your books directly; if you plan on not using a third-party vendor to distribute your books, then this is an option you need to consider.

This section will cover Kindle Direct Publishing, your Amazon Author Spotlight, and KDP promotions. I've also included a note about Amazon's Audible service, and whether you should consider creating an audiobook – I should mention it somewhere.

Create KDP Account

My advice for self-publishing, even if you are going to use someone like Bookbaby or IngramSpark, is to setup your own Kindle Direct Publishing account, rather than going through a third-party. This is essential if you are planning on running a free or discounted Kindle launch, and I've found it useful to have *Do Share Inspire* in my account, where I can easily edit the content.

It also means that if you are thinking of publishing future books, you can manage all of your Kindle titles in one location. Okay, I'm still a little bit of a control freak, but trust me on this one.

Amazon does provide you with a lot of information on how to use their platform to self-publish. Simply go to kdp.amazon.com and click 'Learn how easy it is', under the video. There is not a lot for you to do prior to having the book ready to go, but it's good to have that all setup and ready to go early, removing potential delays.

Note: KDP is Amazon's ebook publishing platform – it allows you to publish Kindle books onto Amazon only. You cannot publish to any other stores or formats through KDP. KDP Select is an exclusivity program within Kindle, which allows you to access sales and promotional functions not available to KDP publishers. I explain more about KDP Select and promotions in a moment.

Complete Your Amazon Author Spotlight

You should also start planning your author page on Amazon now. You will not be able to finalise this until you have a book to claim. When your Kindle or paperback is published onto Amazon, simply go to authorcentral.amazon.com, and set up your account and details on the Author Page.

Note: when your physical book is published, you might have to go back into this site to request it be added to your profile, but if you have already published a Kindle copy, that pairing should happen automatically.

Include as much information as you can in that spotlight, it might be the only time that people ever see you, so have photos, links to your website or blog, relevant videos. This is my Amazon Author page amazon.com/author/kyliedunn, as an example. But check out your favourite authors for more inspiration.

One of the annoying things about Amazon is that all of their country sites are independent of each other. This means, that the Author Spotlight you set up on the US store will not flow through to the UK, Australia, Canada etc. Where you do not have a Spotlight page setup for a country, it will default to a list of books by the same author name – yes, that means they might not be your books. Do not waste time updating your Spotlight in countries where you have no readers, but be prepared to change that if you start getting an audience there.

Plan KDP Select Giveaway/Reduced Price

This is an 'as required' or 'if applicable' task. You may not want to do a Kindle giveaway, but since this is the advice that most self-publishing 'experts' will give you, I thought I should mention it.

The idea is that you can enrol your book in the KDP Select program, which allows you to run a 'free' giveaway, or a reduced price promotion for a period of time.

That sounds simple enough, but there are some things that you should know, because Amazon have put in measures to stop people 'gaming' the system for bestseller status based on free downloads.

- **You have to enrol your book in KDP Select for a minimum of three months** – during that time you cannot be selling your ebook anywhere else; that includes your own website. This is why I've included this step in Stage Two, because you need to think about whether you are going to do this **before** you start the process of publishing an ePub into any other online store.

- **Amazon now has two categories 'Paid' and 'Free'** – any book 'purchased' during the free period will count towards your status in the Free category only. If you start charging for your book, you will start with no sales in the Paid category, and you will need to build your credibility with paid purchases before you can get bestseller paid. By the way, **I think this is entirely fair**, and I can't believe it took so long for them to make the change.

If you are considering a giveaway, you can only run 'free' for five days in any enrolment period; this does not have to be five days in a row. You need to make sure that you have the means of widely publicising the free download period, to get the best results – there are services like BookBub that you can enrol your giveaway in to increase your reach. I'll mention all of this again in marketing.

The other Kindle option is to run at a discounted rate. Again, you can only run this once during the enrolment period, and it can go for a maximum of seven days. You can discount it to a set price for the entire time, say 99c, or you can incrementally increase the price over that time – so day two is $1.49, day three $1.99 etc. At the end of the time period you will be at your original price.

Since you are limited to just Kindle for three months, you might consider doling out the free days to coincide with publicity events, like being on a good podcast. You should avoid chopping and changing from paid to free though, since your sales will take a hit whenever you are in free mode, affecting your overall sales ranking in your category.

You might not consider only having your book on Kindle as a limitation, in fact many people only publish their ebook on Kindle. If that is the case, make sure you enrol in KDP Select so you can take advantage of discounting the book – noting that you cannot discount it without being enrolled in the program. Yes, you can change the price of your book every day in KDP if you wish, but it won't show as a 'discounted price', it will just be the new price.

In short, I'm not saying it's a bad thing to release your book in this way through Kindle, but you need to understand what you're signing up for. You also need to understand that it won't guarantee success, just because it is free it will not sell itself; you'll need just as much promotion for that release, if not more.

A Brief Mention of Audible and Audiobooks

It occurs to me that I have failed to mention the growing market of audiobooks. That is largely because I have not ventured into that area yet, and this book is based around my experiences in self-publishing. I have recorded all of the audio for *Do Share Inspire*, but it will be a little longer before that is stitched together into an audiobook.

The *Book Riot* podcast has shared a lot of facts about the growth in audiobooks throughout 2015, which aligns to a decline in ebooks. It might not be the right fit for your book, but it could be something to consider.

If the thought of doing this yourself is too overwhelming, Amazon has a service that can help. It's called Audiobook Creation Exchange (ACX), and it helps authors and narrators connect with each other, to turn a book into an audiobook. There is even an option to profit-share the publication of the audiobook, rather than paying upfront fees. The *Novel Marketing Podcast* introduced me to this service in Episode 68 – yes there is a link on the resource page; it's a fantastic episode.

As I said, I haven't done this or used the service, but I thought I should mention audiobooks as a possible option in your self-publishing journey. It provides another format, and they are easily published to Amazon's Audible service.

MARKETING AND PROMOTING YOUR BOOK

MAKE SURE YOU KEEP YOUR AUDIENCE, REACH AND FINANCES IN MIND WHEN YOU ARE CONSIDERING HOW TO MARKET YOUR BOOK

This is an area that needs to start during the writing process, and will continue into Stage Five. Remember that this book does not give the sequential steps for writing and launching your book; it would be very disjointed if I organised it that way. The project overview template you can download gives you an outline of timings for these activities – use it to help you plan and schedule these tasks.

Develop Contact List of Desired Media Outlets

This is a step you can start doing now, even if you haven't settled on the exact content for your book. Start getting a list of all of the media outlets you think might be interested in featuring a book on the topic you plan to write. Chances are you already read some of their content, or you listen to a podcast that inspires you on this topic; start writing the list, and keep it handy so you can easily add new ones to it. Consider traditional and non-traditional media:

- Newspapers

- Online news websites

- Radio

- Television

- Podcasts

- Blogs

While you are adding them to the list, include any contact details, or links to their contact rules on the web. As with everything in life, you should avoid having to do the same thing twice for no benefit – if you are looking up the website and seeing how to get in contact, take down the details so you don't have to look it up again later.

Select a Public Relations Company

This is an 'as required' step in the process, although I would recommend that you at least hire someone else to write a press release for you, and maybe even your bio. You might be a great writer, but writing to catch the interest of the press is a special skill; this is a great place to invest a little money.

You should also consider whether you have the time to shop that press release out to the market, or if it's better to spend the money for a PR company to do this for you. Think of it this way:

- A **time poor** self-publisher will benefit from spending money to have someone else do the tasks they don't have time for.

- A **money poor** self-publisher will have the time to learn and undertake the tasks they can't afford to pay someone else to do.

- A **time and money poor** self-publisher is going to struggle and will have to get more creative about getting other people to help in promotion.

Work out which category you fall into, and be realistic about what that means when you start considering marketing.

Select a Press Release Distribution Company

If you fall into the money poor category, you will need to become familiar with the world of online press release distributors – if you're going to pay a PR company then you can ignore this step. There are a lot of companies out there that can distribute your press release; most are paid services, but there are a few that operate for free.

I used PRLog.com as a free service, and apart from having paid services emailing me to inform me about how great their service is, I didn't get any other enquiries. I think it is worthwhile to try the free ones though, you might just hit with the right topic at the right time.

For paid services, they are still generally a lot less than using a PR company to distribute for you. There is a very broad range of prices in this category, depending on whether you are looking to optimise the online presence of your press release, or if you want to use these services to contact traditional newsrooms in newspaper, radio and television.

Ultimately, it is still hit and miss, since your press release is going into a bucket with everyone else. Yes, if you have a great headline and your idea happens to be topical at the moment, you can break through the chaff – but don't count on it. This is only one part of your marketing.

Develop Your Media Kit

So, you should already have an author bio to include in the back of your book; now you have a press release (or two) as well – you're well on your way for your media kit.

The purpose of the media kit is to give journalists, bloggers, podcasters, quick and easy access to information if they want to publicise you, work with you, or even interview you. This media kit should contain the following:

- Author biography – this can be the same as you have in the back of the book, or it could have a little more detail.

- Press Releases – you might want to have more than one. There are always multiple ways to sell a topic, particularly if your book is a complex range of information. Consider a couple of targeted press releases that focus on those angles.

- Sample Q&A – this is really helpful for journalists, because it already provides them with a range of questions and answers around why you wrote the book, who you are, what the aim of the book is etc. It might mean that they can feature you without even having to interview you, or it will be their research. It's best if you can actually get someone who interviews people to do this Q&A, or at a minimum go out to your audience and ask them what they might want to know about you and the book.

- Photos – you should have a couple of photos in your media kit. You definitely need a great head shot, this is something that it is worthwhile paying for – particularly since you should include a head shot in your book, maybe even on the back cover. You might also want a torso or full body shot, for variety. I would also recommend either a casual photo, particularly if the book is about you or is a novel, or a workplace-type photo, if it's on a professional topic.

You should set up a page on your website that is the 'media kit' page. Include downloads of all of these files and make it easy for people to find and access the information.

As you move through promoting and marketing the book, you can also add links on this page to articles, blogs or podcasts that have already featured you. This adds to your credibility and lets them know that you are familiar with the media process, and can carry on an intelligent conversation.

Develop Marketing Strategy/Plan

You need to make sure you have developed a sound strategy/plan for the launch of your book by the post-production stage of the process. There are a few questions your plan should answer, as well as being a consolidated list of dates and actions for the pre-launch and ongoing promotional activities.

What is your goal in publishing this book?

Your goal for this book will drive the sort of marketing options you include in your plan. For example, if this is about selling as many copies as possible, then your marketing strategy has to include a huge amount of promotion – to get in front of as many possible buyers as you can. You'll need to ensure you get reviews, and that influential people talk about your book. If your goal is to publish a book that you can give away, to try and grow your audience, your marketing strategy will focus on websites and services that let readers know about free books. You still want to get in front of a lot of people, but you want to persuade them to sign up to your list – and the bulk of the marketing will be online.

Define the goal, so you can ensure you are selecting options that support that goal.

How you'll measure success

If you are putting time and money into something, you should have a way of evaluating whether you are achieving your goals. For a marketing plan, this should be a set of success metrics that allow you to work out whether the actions you are taking are having the right impact on the goal you want to achieve.

There are a range of measures you can use; these all depend on the goal you wish to achieve. For example, if it's all about becoming a bestselling author, then book sales are going to be the most important indicator of success. You might need some clever tracking codes to work out where online sales are coming from, so you have a chance of identifying which marketing options are achieving the outcome you desire. If the goal is using it to grow an audience, then it's about subscriptions to your website, and knowing which sources are providing the best leads.

Define your measures of success and how you will gather the information – if you have no way of measuring it, it can't be used to define success.

What is your budget, and how will you spend it?

A lot of people self-publish on a small budget, and money is better spent publishing a professional book than placing ads for it. This means you might have a limited budget for promotions. Make sure you are realistic about that budget, and how you might be able to mix unpaid and paid options together for a better outcome. Get creative with these options, and before you pay for anything consider a) whether it is aligned to your goal; b) whether it will achieve what you think; c) whether there is another way of doing it; and d) if you are pursuing the option because you don't know what else to do.

Set the budget and what you are willing to spend money on – and stick to it!

What resources are available to you?

What contacts do you already have that could help you promote the book? This could include:

- audiences you have on your website or social media.
- clients or customers you already work with.
- influential people you already have connections with.
- friends or family members.
- groups, networks or organisations you belong to.

Think of every option – it might be worthwhile to join a network or group three to six months before your book launch, if it aligns well.

Who is your audience, and where do they hang out?

If you play in the online space, you might have heard people talking about 'creating your avatar'. If you don't know what this means, it's basically describing your core reader/audience – we briefly talked about this in Stage 1. The way I've had it explained to me, as part of about five different courses, is that you should create the complete outline of your ideal customer, as an individual person – it helps to give them a full personality and name as well.

The idea is that this person becomes the focus of your writing, and promotions. Yes, other people will see, read and connect with the material; but an avatar ensures you maintain a focus on the messages and the way you approach the audience.

Define your ideal 'reader' and come up with a list of online and offline places they hang out.

What does your audience need to know about the book?

If you hire a PR person, they will help you come up with the messaging, but spend some time working out exactly what your audience might want or need to know about the book. Is there any background they require? Can you do a blog post about that beforehand? What are the themes of the book? What will they learn or discover from it? Why is the story interesting? What makes it unique?

You could do this by asking people in your audience what they would like to know, and asking reviewers what they got out of it. Remember, this is your story; you are so close to it that you'll probably find it difficult to step far enough away to develop the full picture.

What's in it for them? Why should your ideal 'reader' buy and read your book?

The rest of the plan

There are other elements required in your marketing plan, including the tone of promotions, images and colours that you will use, and how much you will share about your life. Most importantly, the plan must have a scheduled checklist of activities. I'm sure you've heard the saying 'failing to plan is planning to fail' – this is true of most things, but doubly true of such an emotional activity, and is new to you.

It's the reason I've given you a project overview, and why I'm developing a more extensive self-publishing toolkit. There is a lot of this that is not intuitive, and there are so many ways you can approach this activity. Failing to have a detailed plan means you are forcing yourself to remember huge amounts of information – trust me when I say that you will not have a lot of brain space when this launches!

Importantly, this detailed schedule should include a content calendar for blog posts you will be publishing (if you do that) and social media content you will be sharing. If you remember the 80/20 rule from earlier, it is very important to create a schedule that ensures every share is not a sales pitch for people to buy your book – 80% others and valuable content vs 20% sales.

Note: the nature of Twitter means you can do more promotion as a percentage, but don't take that too far.

To help you manage that ratio, keep a document or spreadsheet where you can collect interesting content over the time leading up to your launch. This could include:

- Blog posts, podcasts, lists, videos or images on related topics that are not created by you.

- Posts from experts that you reference in your book.

- A TED Talk on a similar or related topic.

- An old blog post you've written on the topic, that does not mention the book.

- Books from other people that you enjoy – these do not need to be related.

- Posts, videos, blogs or podcasts related to other things you do or that might be valuable to your audience.

Consider using the scheduling options of Hootsuite to setup the posts a week in advance, so you are not having to do all of this with the stress of other activities.

Develop your detailed schedule, and stick to it!

Make sure you include a regular review of progress against your goals, so you can make informed decisions about changing the plan, if it's needed.

Select Your Marketing Options

You can start developing ideas for marketing at any point in the writing/editing/production processes, you can even continue to come up with new ones once you are in post-production and your book is selling. Below is a list of activities and products you might wish to consider as part of your marketing strategy/plan outlined above.

Before I start with this list, please remember two things: don't make this more complicated and expensive than it needs to be; and, not all activities will work for you, depending on your genre and audience. Make sure you keep your audience, reach and finances in mind when you are considering the options below.

Design and print marketing products

If you have a physical book, then I would recommend you consider printing some form of marketing material – and since it's a BOOK, then maybe a bookmark is the way to go. Yes, you can get much further reach with an online campaign, but it's great if you have something to give people in person.

Consider printing bookmarks, business cards, postcards or flyers – get them professionally designed, but make sure they have the clear message to check out your book! Make sure you include your website, and maybe an email address (that's up to you).

Create quote images for social media

You've all seen the images with quotes on them that are shared throughout social media. You can create your own, for free, with a range of online tools or phone apps. Pick a couple of relevant quotes from your book, or even quotes about your book; find some relevant images, or take your own photos (smartphones are the best invention for this sort of thing); then join them together and *voila*!

Canva.com is a great free website for this, they even have a range of stock photos and elements you can use for very little money. I use VanillaPen and Over on my iPhone as well, but there are many, many other options available. If you aren't design oriented, ask a friend who is, ask your fans to create some for you, or try a service like Fiverr.

Create a presentation on your content

Visuals are great for sharing, and the colour and movement of a slideshow can work even better. There are two online tools I would suggest sharing a presentation in, one will be more work than the other.

The easier option is Slideshare, which is a free service that's been around for ages, and has recently been bought by LinkedIn. You can create a simple powerpoint presentation about the key points of your book; a brief summary of the main content so people know what they're getting; upload it into Slideshare; then share it on social media. This works well for non-fiction books.

The other option, which is inherently more creative, is a Prezi presentation. Prezis are non-linear presentations that offer a range of effects that I can't do justice to by explaining here. Go to prezi.com and check out some of the presentations to see what's possible. This would work for non-fiction, but probably suits a fictional book more.

Try an online book tour

I'm going to start by saying that I have never done one of these, and I know some people who have done them who weren't overly happy with the results. Basically, there are businesses that will connect you with bloggers and even podcasters, and perform all of the administration to get articles published about you and your book in a set timeframe.

I think they can be quite hit and miss, and they consume a lot of your time – so for the time poor among you don't even think about it. I've heard that for some people they work very well, but I suspect that might be very dependent on genre and the bloggers involved.

Do your own author Q&A

If you already have your own audience, then you could always consider hosting your own Q&A with the Author on a range of free online systems. I wouldn't recommend using a paid webinar service for this, but you could consider something like a Google Hangout (which will also publish the recording to YouTube), or Blab. You could even do a Periscope or Facebook Live event, or series of events – these do have more limited lives though.

Remember to make it interesting and ask questions beforehand, so you have some level of engagement with your audience and are answering what they want to know, not what you think is interesting.

I would not recommend a Twitter #Ask event if there is any possible controversy over your book. The Twitter audience can be quite jaded and cynical – seriously, look up 'EL James Twitter Q&A' on Google to see how bad it can go. This is unlikely to impact you on your first book launch, but you never know.

Create a fan page for the main character

This is for fiction only, but why not bring a character to life so the fans can interact with them in a real way? Go onto Facebook or Twitter and create a page/account for your main character; post content they would enjoy; share pithy comments on the world from their perspective; allow fans to post questions and have conversations with them.

Only do this if you have the time the manage it and keep up with demand. If you are time poor, then you probably don't want to take on the commitment.

Join Goodreads and set up your author page

My sincere hope is that you are a reader, because I do take issue with people trying to write books if they don't read them as well. If you are a reader, then go to Goodreads and set up your author page – yes this can only be done after you have published a book. Goodreads is a wonderful online community of passionate readers, you want to make sure they can find your book and have some way of interacting with you, or finding out more about you if they are interested.

You can link your author page to your blog, and you can also allow readers to ask you questions on that page. Remember, this is a community of readers, so think about what you would like to know as a reader when you engage with them.

You can also pay to promote your book through Goodreads; I haven't done this, but I've heard it can work well for some authors. You should also seriously consider doing a Goodreads giveaway – I did do one of these.

Develop a worksheet or summary of actions

This is for non-fiction only. Consider creating a worksheet or summary sheet that anyone can download and access from your website. This should be designed to accompany the book, but it can also be an effective marketing tool to pique the interest of people who have not read the book – that means you need to make sure you aren't giving too much away in the content.

Have a photo competition

I know a lot of authors that do photo competitions of their books 'in the wild'. Some people like photos of their books in bookshops – which provides them with a great gallery of books on shelves, and might also provide a list of bookshops for potential events. Other authors like to have a competition of people reading their book – this adds that social credibility of showing people who actually bought the book. Depending on your topic, you could have a competition of people doing something from the book as well.

This sort of activity invites your readers to engage with you, and the prize can be something simple and non-expensive as well. Maybe a signed print of an image from the book; the opportunity to meet the author, virtual or in person; a signed copy of another book or the next book; or other merchandise you might create based on the book (see Create POD Merchandise below).

Create incentives for fans

What do I get for sharing your book with my friends and followers? Think about incentives you can offer your fans to get them to share your book – or better still, review it! This could be access to you; signed copies of something; a mention on your platform; writing an article for their blog; talking to their book club; or other merchandise you might create based on the book (see Create POD Merchandise below).

Yes, it is lovely when people are so happy with your work that they want to share or review it without any prompting, but remember that everyone is pretty busy nowadays. Sometimes a little nudge will help remind them to take that action.

A quick note on reviews

I think this is a great time to mention that you should never 'buy' reviews from people. There are some services you can use, I'll mention one a little later, that allow people to download a free copy of your ebook in the hope they will provide you with an Amazon review – but that is as close as you should get to paying for a review.

Amazon has recently started cracking down on reviews that are obviously from paid sources, or done through some group bartering system. By this I mean, say you're part of a Facebook writing group and you all agree to give each other a review of your books – glowing reviews that are given without the person necessarily having read the book. There are 10 of you, so you'll each start with nine reviews. Apparently Amazon is now cross-matching these reviews, and removing suspicious content.

Reviews have to be earned, and they have to be honest – you actually want the odd two or three-star review, because most people don't believe something is perfect, so they want to know which part of this might be disappointing. It doesn't mean they won't buy it, actually it can mean quite the opposite.

Give free copies to places your readers might go

If you have a physical book, then you are going to have to be prepared to give copies away. This will include copies to reviewers, people who have helped out, influencers, bloggers, podcasters and a number of other people. You might want to start considering other places to gift a copy of your book as well. The idea is to find places your audience might go, and see if they would like a free copy of the book. Places like:

- libraries – local and state
- schools
- coffee shops
- B&Bs or small hotels
- senior citizen centres
- advocacy and support offices
- prisons
- universities.

Make sure that you include information in the front of the free copy about where they can buy a copy of their own, or at a minimum sign up for your newsletter and more details.

Do book readings at places your readers might go

This is like the point above, but rather than leaving a free copy of the book, you might want to consider doing book readings or short talks about why you wrote the book. Again, consider options like:

- libraries
- schools
- bookshops
- senior citizen centres
- universities
- book clubs
- related business networking groups or associations.

Create POD merchandise

Again, make good use of the print-on-demand economy. You can use online stores like Redbubble or Society6 (there are heaps more), to create print-on-demand products like t-shirts, stickers, mugs, and smartphone cases. This means there is no initial outlay for you and, like a POD book, you don't have to worry about shipping.

Think about artwork of your characters, or their favourite sayings; putting quotes of the book on mugs or tote bag; maybe even the book cover on a tote bag. Get creative, and you may have an entire range of products for fans to purchase – you might also get people who find the products and then become fans of the book.

Promoting your free/sale Kindle book

I mentioned earlier about considerations for doing ebook promotions through KDP Select. There are a number of sites that you can use to publicise that promotion, BookBub is probably the main player, but they are a paid service with restriction on the books they will promote.

When I was doing my recent free promotion to reinvigorate my first ebook, I came across two great blog posts on the topic that you should read (links are in your resources as well):

- 47 places to submit your free KDP promotion – find this article at trainingauthors.com

- Maximise your KDP Select free days – find this article at digitalbooktoday.com.

Be a blog or podcast guest

One of the ways of increasing your audience and reach is to be featured on a popular blog or podcast. In Stage Five I've included specific details about finding and pitching bloggers and podcasters, so you should refer to that for the detail.

Writing a guest post for a blog, or being a guest on a podcast, allows you to share your knowledge or story with a new audience. The aim is to intrigue them, or provide them with something so valuable that they will want more from you. This could be subscribing to become part of your audience, or buying your book.

It is a no cost marketing option, as long as you have the time to create content, or participate in an interview for the podcast. There are many options available for this, I've included some references on your resource page dinkylune.com/wtlstuff.

Should You Crowdfund Your Book?

> YOU CAN'T THINK OF IT AS THE SIMPLE WAY TO FUND YOUR BOOK, BECAUSE IT TAKES A LOT OF TIME AND EFFORT TO HUSTLE A CROWDFUNDING CAMPAIGN

It would be remiss of me not to briefly touch on crowdfunding as a promotional tool, as well as a way to help fund your publishing journey. I start this by saying that I have not crowdfunded anything. I have supported campaigns; read a lot about the experience; and assisted someone with the process – but this is not my own experience here.

If you don't know what crowdfunding is, or if you are only vaguely familiar; there are a range of online services (such as Kickstarter,

Indigogo and Pozible) that allow you to run a campaign to get people to invest in your product or event. They invest before it is a thing, so you can have the capital to make it a thing. For their investment, they will receive a 'reward', which you define as part of the campaign – books often include signed copies of the book as the most common reward, although you can include shout-outs on your site, eternal devotion, promotional products (shirts, mugs, etc), original artwork, or even 'meet the author'.

A campaign will usually run for three to four weeks, although it is fair to say that the majority of people will not sign up until the last couple of days – this is a quirk of human nature that can be maddening for something like this. You have make your campaign information compelling and creative; there are some fantastic videos that have been created for crowdfunding campaigns. They are not a quick and easy way to fund your creative project, and the campaigns that make six to seven figures are few and far between.

The way it works is, you set a total that you want or need to reach; let's say $2,500 to help with editing and design. You create a range of rewards, and people sign up for the reward they want to receive. If you sell enough rewards to reach $2,500 or more, payments are made, the site takes its commission and you receive the remainder. But if you fail to reach your $2,500 target, no payments are made, and you receive nothing. So it is not 'guaranteed' money, which is why I say it's a lot of work to make sure you get over the line. And yes, if you set a $2,500 goal and people end up investing in $5,000 worth of rewards, you get the additional funds.

The 'expert' advice seems to be that crowdfunding is a great way to generate buzz about your book, and get a lot of pre-sales; as well as funding to support publishing and printing. So let's break that down.

- Generating buzz – this is only true if you have an audience to get buzzing. Creating a crowdfunding campaign is not a quick task. So many creative ventures now use crowdfunding, so you need to put effort into standing out in the crowd. Your campaign has to be compelling; your rewards have to be valuable enough for people to commit; and your expectations need to be realistic, or you might end up with nothing. You can't think of it as the simple way to fund your book, because it takes a lot of time and effort to hustle a crowdfunding campaign – sometimes more than launching the book.

- Pre-sales – yes, if you make a copy of the book (or copies) part of your rewards, then you will get pre-sales of the book. That means that you know you have an audience ready to go when the book is done, which must be a weight off. It is vital that you remember that you are going to have to distribute all of these copies yourself – so if you happen to get 100 pre-sales in the crowdfunding, you will need to package all of these up and mail them off. And you will need to meet all of the other rewards as well. Just don't get too excited about pre-sales and money up front when you are preparing your crowdfunding rewards; remember how much time and money it will take to deliver them. That means, calculate postage and packaging in your reward offerings; offer an ebook as a low cost option (if that's appropriate); and think about how much time each of those funky rewards will take.

- Funding the project – if you are cash-poor but time-rich, this might be a great option for you to take. You could crowdfund your editor and designers; if you aren't doing print-on-demand it's also a great way to help fund the cost of printing and shipping 1,000+ copies of your book to you. But you also need to be realistic about how much funding you can generate for your project, with your audience. How many $5–$25 rewards do you have to get people to sign up for to reach the funding you require? And is that feasible? And remember, you still need to deliver the rewards at the end. So if you managed to get $2,500 in your crowdfunding, but you will need to mail out 100 copies of the book, how much of this do you need to set aside for postage and packaging? How much is actually available for you to readily use to complete the book? Are you really just shifting the stressful lack of funds issue to the end of the process – but now you've added a commitment to 100 people that you cannot meet?

I don't want this to be doom and gloom, but you need to think about these things.

Am I saying you shouldn't do it?

Of course I'm not! What I'm saying is that you should not consider it a silver-bullet that will give you an income to write your book, all of the funds you require to get it created, and all the funds to market it. Sure, if you are already a highly paid consultant, and you can offer rewards that do not include copies of the book, then you have greater flexibility – but if that's you then you might not need crowdfunding.

And for me that is the point, crowdfunding is a great option when you don't **need** it. It is a great way to get people buzzing; to get them invested in the publishing of your book; to let them feel like they are insiders in your creative process; and to build an audience that is anticipating the books release. But as a means of funding a process that you cannot afford to undertake for yourself? Well there can be some serious issues to consider.

As I noted above, you could end up losing money on a crowdfunding campaign – it has happened to more than one person. You need to be rational and reasonable. I know you're going to want to offer people the world to get them into the campaign, but resist that urge. You need to convince them that they want to help you turn this book into a reality, rather than offering them brilliant deals to get in early – this is a community that wants kudos for supporting you, not unrealistic discounts, remember that.

I thought about crowdfunding *Do Share Inspire* – for about a minute. The reasons I decided not to do it are important. I was working to an unrealistic timeframe, and did not have time and energy to devote to a crowdfunding campaign. So, I felt my time was better spent trying to build the promotion for the launch, rather than pre-launch buzz.

More importantly though, I had the means to do this without crowdfunding, and if I'd failed to meet my target I would have published the book anyway. I think this is a significant point to note: I felt it would be disingenuous of me to go out to my community and ask them to help me get this done, and if I failed to reach the target, turn around two months later and publish it anyway.

Crowdfunding has its place, and it can work very effectively – but make sure you know exactly what you are getting yourself into.

Stage Three – Making it a Book

Before we get into the nitty-gritty of this stage, you need to make a decision about what sort of self-publishing option you intend to use. There are three quite different options available to you, and once you select which one you will use, it will help you understand how much of this chapter you really need. This brief overview does not consider every aspect of these options, just the most salient points.

I wanted to take a moment to mention 'vanity publishers', because the ability to pay someone to publish your book is not new to the digital world. For decades, a small number of publishers gave writers the ability to pay a fee to 'publish' their book, often with costly clauses that forced authors to overpay for the actual services delivered.

To some degree, the world of self-publishing is an extension of the vanity press situation, particularly if you use a full-service publishing house. There is a distinct difference though, since vanity publishers often required authors to purchase large numbers of books, or some other inflated service they offered. The growth of true self-publishing, has allowed some vanity publishers to market themselves as 'viable' options, so be aware of the conditions and clauses of a company that offers to do it all. Remember, it is quite cost effective to self-publish, and you should have flexibility in the services and options you use.

I PREFER THE POD MODEL BECAUSE IT'S COST EFFECTIVE, GIVES ME THE MOST CONTROL, IS LESS RISKY AND HAS GREAT ONLINE DISTRIBUTION

Full-service publishing – there are a range of self-publishing services that 'do it all' for you. Balboa Press is one of these types of publishers. If you want to check out their 'packages' it will give you a better idea of what I mean. If the idea of getting your own ISBNs; hiring cover and internal designers; hiring PR people; and a range of other tasks, seems too daunting, you could consider these types of vendors. They usually have a range of packages that add in various services. Points to note:

- Packages usually include an ISBN – remember what I said earlier about who owns it, and pay attention to what rights you are giving away to the publisher.

- Some of the services they include are made to sound more complex than they are.

- Few will provide an editing service, so that is still something you need to arrange.

- The royalty rate is generally a little lower than the POD vendors.

- Often, you lose some control in the process, and may not have access to all of your original files to move away from that vendor if you aren't happy.

- You will probably find that if you looked for your own cover designer, get your own ISBN etc, it would be cheaper than the majority of their packages.

- Lastly, from my research, their marketing packages leave a lot to be desired – so don't get caught up in thinking they will 'sell' your book, no one will do that but you!

Print-on-demand vendors – while the full-service providers also offer a POD service for the books, there are a lot of differences between them and POD vendors, who are companies that will print/distribute your book/ebook to the world. Some of them do offer a range of services that you can purchase, like the full-service publishers, but all of them allow you to strip that back and simply use them as a printer/distributor. These include companies like IngramSpark, CreateSpace and BookBaby. Points to note:

- There is a lot of variety in what these businesses offer and how they charge. I've included a little more on the main players in the Print Production section.

- There can be limitations in their distribution channels, which means more work for you in Stages 4 and 5.

- The ebook distribution channels can also vary, but I recommend doing Kindle on your own anyway.

- Ingram (or LightningSource) is used as the POD vendor for many full-service publishers.

Printing companies – you can, of course, go entirely outside print-on-demand, and go to a traditional printer to get 500+ copies of your book printed; 1,000 is often the minimum. If you are only intending on selling them yourself, through an online store or in person, and you have the money upfront to fund printing and storage costs, this option could work. Points to note:

- Because you are buying in bulk, the per unit cost of each book is likely to be significantly less than a POD book.

- You need to make sure you have space to store the books; don't underestimate how much room they will take up.

- You should factor mailing into your costs, and the time it might take to service orders. Note: you can probably still engage a distributor to organise that aspect for you, at a price.

- If you want to publish as an ePub, you will still have to look at the online providers – you can do Kindle yourself of course.

This book has been written under the assumption that you are planning to use a POD vendor. While large sections of the content are still valid regardless of which of the three options you have selected, I am not including specific information on how to work with full-service or printing companies – largely because I have never used them.

I prefer the POD model of publishing for the following reasons:

- I'm pretty tech savvy, so there is a lot of this I can do myself – making it more cost effective.

- I like to have as much control as possible, including making changes as and when I need them – do not underestimate this element. I have made a number of minor corrections to *Do Share*

Inspire, and rewritten the entire back cover. I would have had to 'live with' those minor, and not so minor, errors if I had done a 1,000 book print run.

- I don't have a huge amount of money to outlay upfront, particularly after the other costs are taken into account.

- I also prefer not to take the risk of storing a large number of books, and have the responsibility for filling orders.

- The distribution is quite extensive, and if I spend time going out to bookstores they can still buy it from the POD vendor.

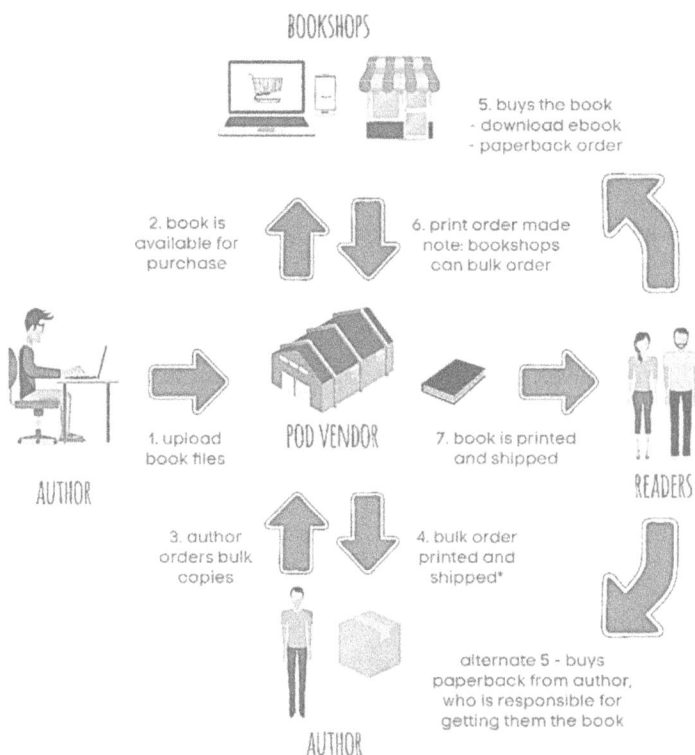

BOOKSHOPS

5. buys the book
- download ebook
- paperback order

2. book is available for purchase

6. print order made note: bookshops can bulk order

1. upload book files

POD VENDOR

7. book is printed and shipped

AUTHOR

READERS

3. author orders bulk copies

4. bulk order printed and shipped*

alternate 5 - buys paperback from author, who is responsible for getting them the book

AUTHOR

Figure 2 - POD Publishing Process - how does it get from my computer to a reader?

Note: full-service publishing is much like Figure 2, except the vendor does the book files as part of their service. When using a printing company, the author moves to the middle and is now responsible for: making the book available to online and offline stores; storing the 1,000+ copies of the book; and shipping all orders.

EDITING YOUR MANUSCRIPT

Just because you are self-publishing, it doesn't mean it should be unprofessional. There are traditionally published authors that have moved into self-publishing to gain greater control over the process and product (James Altucher and Seth Godin come to mind). It means you have complete control, but it does not mean you get to slap something together and publish it.

This is particularly true if you are planning to use this book as a business card, or to ensure you are seen as an expert. A poorly edited, designed and laid out book will not do that for you!

What type of editing do you need?

There are two types of editing you should consider for your book; high level and low level editing:

- Developmental Editing – this is a high level editing process that looks at the structure of your book and whether content needs to be reorganised, removed or added to make your book flow for the reader. Again, since you are so close to the topic you might not be able to see the gaps or the disconnect in content flow, so it's useful to have a developmental editor review your manuscript before a copyeditor looks at it.

- Copyediting – this is the line by line, low level editing of your manuscript to make sure that the copy (or content) is accurate, standardised and correct. There is an element of proofreading in this, but copyeditors will also look at the structure of sentences and paragraphs to make sure they are comprehensible. There might be some minor rewriting at this stage.

Selecting an editor

Go online and find an editor who has some experience with your genre. My advice is to do a Google search for your local editors' association, ask other people who you know have used an editor for recommendations, or enquire with a local writers' association.

Once you have a shortlist, ask for details of recent work they've done, including contact details for at least one person. Also, get a quote for editing your book; you'll need to talk about genre and word length with them. Lastly, if you can meet them, or at least talk to them, do that so you can get a feel for them and their interest in your work. I think the editor needs to have at least a basic interest in your work to do a good job.

When you have chosen an editor, you should consider setting up a contract with them. They might have a contract for the service they provide, and that's great, but you want to make sure they sign a non-disclosure on your manuscript. It's just a safeguard, I'm sure I will never need to use it, but it's nice to have.

Editor corrections

When you hand over your manuscript, ensure that you have an agreed date for the corrections to come back, and an understanding about what you will get with that service. It's important to remember that you do have the ultimate say in your content as the corrections are suggestions only – which means that you should get your manuscript returned marked up, with tracked changes. Now, since you are paying a professional for their advice and experience, I would not recommend that you reject these corrections without a clear reason for doing so – chances are they are right and you need to not be precious about it.

Once you receive the editor's corrections, go through and look at what the changes are before you accept them. It is possible for the editor to completely change the meaning of your writing, if it was a little confusing in the first instance and they took a guess. Make sure you are happy that the meaning and intent has remained the same before you accept those corrections.

Proofreading by non-professionals

It's great if you have a number of friends who are happy to read the book, provide commentary and maybe even proofread for you – but this should not be in lieu of using a professional editor. I would use these people after the professional editing process is complete; they can help validate the decisions you might have made in structure and content, as well as picking up errors that might have slid past an editor.

Your editor may miss things; I probably should have mentioned this before. Editing is a very detailed task, and the human brain is a great auto-corrector. I don't think I've ever purchased a book without at least one typo in it, and that includes traditionally published books that go through the wringer in editing and proofing. So having a small group of people who can read through it with fresh eyes when it is 99% there is a great idea.

To index or not to index?

This is for non-fiction authors only. Do you plan on indexing your book? If your book is 20–30,000 words long, there is probably no need to do it. If it is broken down into simple chapters that are topic specific, again probably not worthwhile. If it is 60,000+ words, and contains a range of themes and topics all wound together that you want people to be able to use as a reference, maybe you should index it.

I didn't index *Do Share Inspire*, even though it is over 120,000 words. I felt that as a memoir based self-help book it was not needed – I could be wrong but with my timeframe there would have been no chance to have the book properly indexed anyway.

If you make the decision to index, I would recommend seeking a professional to do this as it is a specialised job – unless you are planning on indexing at a very high level, in which case you may be able to do that yourself.

Note: indexing is not as relevant in the ebook world, since there are search functions. I would not recommend spending money to index an ebook for that reason.

DESIGNING THE COVER

Alongside the editing process, you need to start working out your cover design. If you are publishing an ebook, you only need to worry about the front cover; physical books require a front cover, spine and back cover.

Publishing a physical book means you need to know the size of your book before your cover can be completed. If you have not decided on the dimensions of the book at this stage, you need to make that decision before you start this section. If you know the height and width dimensions but you're not entirely sure of the page count yet, that's not too problematic – but you need to let your designer know you don't have the spine width yet, as they can't finalise the cover until they have that.

If you think that having a good book cover doesn't matter, you're delusional! The saying 'you can't judge a book by its cover' is completely true – but that saying exists because that is exactly what we do as human beings. If your cover is unprofessional, people will assume that your book is also unprofessional – possibly poorly written or not edited well. You're putting all of this effort into producing a good book; give it the wrapper it deserves.

Select and brief the cover designer

You may be fortunate enough to have a graphic artist/designer in your life, if so that's a great place to start. Remember though that designing business logos and letterhead is not necessarily the same as designing a book cover; have a discussion with them about that process before you go with them.

If you don't have a go-to person for this (and your 17-year-old nephew who knows how to use Illustrator is probably not the go-to person), shop around. Ask other people for recommendations; go onto Fiverr or 99designs and find someone online; or speak to local graphic design companies.

Note: discuss up front what the deliverables will be. Ask for the editable design files so you have the flexibility to have small changes made – some designers will not do this, but it never hurts to ask.

If you've ever had a logo or brand design done before, you'll understand what briefing a designer means. You don't just say to the designer, 'here is the book title, it's about marketing' and hope for the best. You need to give them as much relevant information as possible. This should cover things like:

- Overview of the book and content.

- Your target audience/demographic.

- Title and subtitle.

- Any current branding for your business – so they understand the font and feeling of your design.

- Tone of the book – light, funny, professional, formal etc.

- Any design elements you want included – maybe you would like a particular photo or illustration included (of course this would be an image you have copyright permission to use).

Most designers will probably send you a questionnaire to complete, or have a meeting with you to discuss all of these elements. Be prepared to let them know what is important to you in the design; it is your book after all.

Note: it's perfectly acceptable to give them a couple of other book covers to show them ideas or the 'feel' you are looking for, but **never say 'I want it to look like this'.** *That's not how design works; book covers are covered by copyright law.*

Importantly, you should have the back cover copy ready to go when you start your cover design. The amount of words, and what is included, might drive certain design decisions – you don't want to try to cram it in at the end.

Back cover copy

So your front cover design is interesting enough for people to pick up the book. Now the back cover (or inside cover if it is a wrapped hardcover book) needs to tell them why they should read it. This is where I get to admit that I got it wrong when I first published *Do Share Inspire*; worse still is the admission that I knew it was the wrong way to go, but I pushed it through anyway.

Here is the first back cover copy for my book, see if you can spot the obvious problem:

'I like to call myself a <u>recovering</u> judgemental, perfectionist control freak – I won't tell you when I last relapsed.'

Even with two failed marriages and a couple of career changes under her belt, Kylie was still striving for perfection – making it easy for her internal critic to harshly judge every mistake and failure.

A few months after her 39th birthday, Kylie started a self-designed project called My Year of TED. It was her attempt to regain control of her life through 21 TED-inspired 30-day activities. Kylie didn't realise it at the time, but she was setting out on her own Yellow Brick Road to find the wisdom to understand herself, the compassion to reconnect, the courage to change, and a way home.

Do Share Inspire is a collection of blog posts from that year and some of the subsequent adventures. It shares a surprisingly honest story of taking inspirational ideas from TED Talks to create practical activities, which unravelled her life and reshaped it via a rollercoaster journey of amazing insights, painful realisation, significant change and eventually, greater happiness.

Do you see it? The cover is all about me and why I did My Year of TED – how does the reader know what they will get from the book?

My advice is to find someone who is a professional copywriter, someone who does back cover copy for a living. Okay, I know you wrote a book, but can you summarise it into a catchy 150 words that will make someone want to buy it? If the answer is yes, great! You'll save yourself a couple of hundred dollars. If you're unsure, spend the money on a professional.

This is the new back cover copy for *Do Share Inspire*, the copy that tells a reader why they might want to read the book:

Do you want to regain control of your life?

Know something needs to change but aren't sure what?

Feel like you're not allowed to change?

Then *Do Share Inspire* is your book.

Kylie Dunn radically transformed her ordinary days by watching more than 350 TED talks; taking ideas from 54 of the best; and applying that brilliance in her life. She'll show you how to do the same through 21 TED inspired activities that will bring you the confidence and clarity to:

- Discover your authentic self

- Find greater happiness in every moment

- Realise you're so much more powerful than you believe

- Gain the courage to make life-altering changes

- Become a stellar decision maker

- Step away from everyone else's expectations of you

- Unravel your negative perceptions of yourself

This isn't one woman's journey, it's your journey too. If you've ever felt forgettable, unlovable, uninteresting ... all that is about to change. Get ready. You're about to go on the transformational adventure of a lifetime.

I knew that this is what the book needed, but I couldn't bring myself to write that – it's like writing your own bio. Some people are comfortable talking about themselves like this, and owning their knowledge; I'm not one of those people.

Drafts and resubmits

It is extremely unlikely that you will get the perfect cover from the first iteration of designs; you should get a range of design options from the first drafts. Your job is to provide the designer with feedback on all of the designs, so they can narrow it down and give you a cover you love.

It's not enough to say 'I don't like number one, and I think number two is boring, so I guess something like number three'. You need to tell the designer what you don't like about particular designs, and what you do like about them as well. Sometimes this is difficult to explain, good design evokes feelings and sometimes it's simply that you don't like the feeling it evokes – great! That feedback is better than 'I don't like it'.

Provide as much feedback as you can, and any additional suggestions that you might have come up with while reviewing the options. Often we are better able to explain what we want when we have something to compare it against; having a few possible designs might make it easier for you to describe a vision you have.

Note: this is like taking editing advice. They might be design professionals, and you should listen to their design expertise, but this is your book. Do not let them drive a 'design' you feel does not align with your book or your brand. Keep an open mind, but use a respected friend or colleague to bounce the designs off if you feel the designer is heading down the wrong path – preferably someone who has read the book.

Depending on your contract with the designer, you might only get one iteration with drafts and feedback. That means that when the cover designs are resubmitted, unless there are errors, you need to pick one. My advice is to have a contract that allows at least two iterations, but that is likely to cost more; a cover is important, but don't make it too important.

Ask your audience

Remember when you were picking a title I mentioned that it's a great time to engage with your audience to get them involved in your book – well the book cover is an even better time to do that. Take the front cover options from the second or third round and ask your audience which one they prefer.

You can do this through a blog post, asking for comments; using an online polling tool; or through social media. Asking them for their input will engage them in your book, and start creating buzz about the book being real. Importantly, it will also help you step back and consider the design from your readers' perspective – after all, you are not the audience for your book!

Finalise the cover

Once you have selected the final cover, you need to get the final design files. For the ebook, this is just a front cover – see if you can get the editable Illustrator, Photoshop or other design file, and not only the finalised JPG image (as mentioned earlier this might not be possible).

For the physical book, you cannot finalise the cover until you have the exact spine width. Once you have finalised the interior of the book (next section), you can work with the cover designer to finalise these files. You will need to ensure that the designer gives you with the files as your publisher or printer requires them – this will be on their website. The simplest way of doing this is to give the designer a link to the requirements, so there is no confusion in translation.

Mock-up cover

It is also worthwhile talking to your designer about a mock-up cover – a three-dimensional cover image that you can use on your website and other promotional content. These images are very popular as they turn a flat 'cover' into a real 'book' – even when that book is only an ebook.

If you are doing this yourself, I've recently discovered a fantastic site with Photoshop mockups that you can use, for free! It's called Covervault (covervault.com) and I've used one of Mark's images for *Do Share Inspire* – it's in the back of this book.

DESIGNING THE INTERIOR

It is essential to have a cover that entices your reader to buy the book, but good design and readability doesn't stop there. The interior design of your book can be as important to the content, as the content itself. If you're publishing a novel, this is quite simple, since there is a fairly uniform structure to the layout of a novel – but non-fiction can be something else entirely.

Which font should you use? Where should the headings go? Stylistically, how do you include lists and examples to support the tone and flow of your book? It's not as simple as it might appear.

Select and brief the book interior designer

I will start by saying, it is not essential for you to have a designer for the interior of your book, if:

- You are publishing a novel OR you are publishing a non-fiction book that does not require distinct design elements, or contain a lot of images

- AND you have excellent Word skills, and know how to apply Styles and structured formatting to your documents.

That means you should strongly consider hiring a designer if:

- You don't know what I mean by applying Styles and structured formatting in Word.

- You are publishing a book with a lot of images.

- You are publishing a non-fiction book with distinct design elements – by this I mean that you are going to include breakout boxes with stories or quotes; you have more complex elements like tables and formulas; or you plan on using a variety of fonts.

Note: there are ways to include some complex design elements in ebooks, but the design of the e-reading applications means they are much easier to read without these elements – and there can be limitations with fonts. Discuss this with your designer; it might mean that the look and feel of the ebook is different, and that you focus more on the physical book design.

See the notes on selecting a cover designer above. This should be the same sort of process, although I would say you want to question them about their experience with print and electronic books, if you are publishing both.

Once you have selected someone, it is best for you to supply a couple of chapters of your book for them to use on the layout concepts. You are not required to give them fully copyedited chapters at this stage, as there are still a number of decisions before they need finalised content.

You should also be providing the designer with a brief, much like the cover process. The designer needs to understand whether you have any preferences for fonts and colours, if you plan on any elements being distinct from the main text, and if there are any other design elements you require. Again, you can consider sending them examples of book layouts you like; while you cannot copyright a book layout, avoid copying one entirely – unless it is a standard design.

Drafts and resubmits

Once the designer has your brief and the sample chapters, they should give you a couple of layout options to consider. Remember that they are the professionals, unless you are getting your cousin Sally who works for a lawyer but is a 'whizz on Word' to do the work for you, which might not be the best option. As professionals, designers understand how to create tone and flow through the use of fonts, colours and white space – but it is still your book. If you feel they have missed the mark in the tone they have created, or you feel it is not easy to read and follow, let them know how you feel about it.

Basically, this process is exactly like the cover design – because it's a design task, and they are all quite similar. Give detailed feedback on the elements you like, and the ones you don't like, from the first round of submissions. Remember to be as descriptive as you can be about it: it might be that you don't like a certain font, but it's better to be able to explain why – 'it's too formal for the feel of the book', or 'it's too similar to every other book'.

Note: it's important to remember that designs can be similar for the simple reason that the design works. When you pick up a novel you expect to find a chapter heading or number, and then pages of uninterrupted text filled out to the margins. We're used to reading novels in this way, and that familiarity means it's approachable to us. If you decide to do something out of the ordinary, you might be putting a barrier between your reader and the content you are trying to share – innovation is not always a good thing.

The designer should take your feedback from the first round of designs, and create a second round for you – unless there was an option in the first round that hit the mark. Hopefully, you were able to articulate your likes and dislikes from the first round well enough that you now have something that will work for you.

Proofing the interior

Once you agree on the interior, you need to give the designer the finalised manuscript – that is the manuscript that has gone through the copyediting and initial proofreading process. The designer will format that content according to your agreed design, and provide you with proofs for review.

It is essential that you completely review these proofs, because sometimes it's not easy for the designer to see 'what' the content is from your manuscript – is that piece of text supposed to be a sub-heading or a stylised quote? Was that text supposed to be italicised, or was that a carry-over from the previous paragraph? What you thought was obvious when you, the editor, and other proof-readers went through the content, may not be by the end of that process.

You might also notice something about the design you thought worked well, but with all of the content now formatted you notice that it's a little clunky or messy in parts. Mark up any corrections or changes that need to be made, and give those comments back to the designer.

The designer should make the required changes and give you a second proof for review. Focus on the changes you asked to be made, but it is also worthwhile to go through the entire proof again – just to be sure. You should also have someone else review the second proof as you are likely to be so familiar with the content now that your brain is seeing what it expects to see.

Finalise the interior

If there are more changes required from the second proof, let your designer know – you should have the ability to go back and forth for corrections until it is right at no extra cost. Remember, that changing your mind about something is not a correction!

Ensure that you get the finalised interior in the format required by your print-on-demand service, which is usually a PDF. I would encourage you to also get it as an editable document – either in Word, InDesign or whatever package was used. Remember, if you are creating an ebook you are going to need a format that your ebook developer can easily use – more on that in the eBook Production section.

BOOK PUBLISHERS

This is where we get to some crossover points. As you will have noticed in the project overview this step starts before all of the editing and design work – because you need to know your vendor's requirements before you can finalise the design.

I've grouped the tasks together here to make it easier to understand, but remember that you should follow the steps laid out in the project overview as **this book is not sequential**.

Selecting a print-on-demand vendor

As mentioned, this book assumes you are using the print-on-demand (POD) style of publishing your book. I explained earlier in this chapter why I think this is a great way to approach self-publishing, hopefully you agree. If you have decided to use a full-service publishing company, one that does your cover design, interior layout, etc, then you already know that most of this chapter is not for you.

If you are going to a printer to get 1,000+ copies of your book, then you need to know their requirements as well at this time. Make sure you understand exactly how they expect the files to be delivered, and the proof and review procedures before you engage them.

We're going to discuss some of the POD vendor options that are available to you. This is not a comprehensive list, and there are new players coming into the market all the time. Below are a couple of the most popular and well-known options you could consider.

IngramSpark.com – they provide POD and ebook distribution services, which include Amazon. So you can use them as a one-stop shop to get your book into all the major online bookstores, as a paperback and/or ebook. Unlike many other services, they do charge you a fee to setup your book – it's US$25 for setup and to upload changes. That's not outlandish, and they don't take as much in commission for each copy purchased, so I figure it all comes out in the wash. Completing all of their tax paperwork is a little tedious though, particularly as a non-resident alien.

- I found their price per book to be very competitive and, as an absolute bonus for me, one of their printers is in Australia. This means I can work with them in Australian dollars (reducing costs) and postage prices are **_significantly_** cheaper. They also have UK and US printers, so if I did need to send a bulk lot somewhere overseas, I can change options to make it more cost effective.

- The quality of the POD books is very good as well; overall I've been very happy with the service and end product. (Note: I don't use them for Kindle distribution, I do KDP myself.)

Amazon.com – by this I mean Kindle Direct Publishing and CreateSpace. I did seriously consider this option, but then I would have had to use another service for the ePub market, and apparently the distribution of CreateSpace printed books is limited. Having said that, they were the cheapest per unit in my research, being a little cheaper than IngramSpark, and having no setup fees. I've also heard that the print quality is quite good, although some comments say it isn't to IngramSpark's standards.

- I would have had to pay in US dollars (our exchange rate is currently crap), and the international postage costs would have eaten up any per unit savings very rapidly.

- The ebook compensation to authors through Kindle is one of the lowest I've seen, but you really can't avoid putting your book on Amazon, so you will have to deal with this regardless.

- In relation to tax issues, their online process for completing a W–8BEN makes the process incredibly simple, particularly as a non-resident alien. I think more online publishers should sort out their processes and follow the Amazon example.

Bookbaby.com – while they offer pretty much the full range of services, they're split out, so you can pick and choose to use them as the printer/distributor of your book, or for everything. I seriously considered them for _Do Share Inspire_, but their print prices were more expensive, and the shipping was ludicrous – but this is the case with most overseas publishers. Unfortunately, books weigh a lot and take up a lot of space, so this can be a significant factor in your decision making.

- There is no setup fee for Bookbaby, and my interactions with their sales team were very positive, but in the end we were talking about well over $1 difference in the unit price with conversion rates and postage (yes, that's a lot).

Lulu.com – I've used them for a few of my books, largely the Do-Pad because they do spiral binding (which is expensive so I don't recommend it). I've always found them quite easy to work with, they take a set price per copy of your book (99c US) not a percentage of the price, so you can manage your revenue well.

- Their distribution is quite limited. While they will place your ePub into Apple's iBookstore and Barnes & Noble, you need to deal with Amazon yourself (print and ebook), which means that Amazon sales are completely up to you to manage.

Smashwords.com – this is an ebook-only publisher, which has wider distribution than Lulu, but it can't do POD. It is also very easy to use, and you keep a good percentage of the revenue. Again, you'll publish in ePub format, but the book will also go to Kobo, the Sony Reader Store, Aldiko and the diesel eBook store, as well as Apple's iBookstore and Barnes & Noble.

- Since they don't do print or Kindle, you would need to consider how many vendors you want to deal with.

A last note on picking a vendor

There are other providers out there. Just do an online search and you will find hundreds of people to help you self-publish. All I will say is buyer-beware – regardless of what type of service you choose make sure you know:

- What rights you are giving away to them.
- How much it will cost you (per unit, including shipping) to get copies of your book.

- What your revenue will be.

- What all the 'additional' charges are.

- How and when they will pay you your royalties.

Know and follow their rules

This is one of the most important steps to follow, especially if you are going to be using the online converter to ePUB format. When I published my first ebook, I looked at the formatting rules for three sites, and the rules were slightly different for all three – yay for standardised formatting!

Each vendor will provide you with instructions about the formatting requirements for uploading your book to their site – physical and ebook. Download their requirements document and follow the rules; if you are using a professional to do any of this work for you, make sure they follow the rules, and are required to fix up any technical errors free of charge to you.

The vendor may also have rules around other things like titling your book, author and publisher details, ISBN requirements, and a number of other minor details. Make sure that you follow these directions, otherwise it could get very frustrating and will introduce delays.

Yes, I am speaking from experience here. Lulu requires you to capitalise each word in the title of your book before it can be distributed to other stores (except the minor ones like a, an, the, of, from etc). I had overlooked this requirement, which didn't stop my book from being published on Lulu.com. However, it has delayed the approval for publication to the iBookstore and Barnes & Noble, which is frustrating. Worse still, I have an oversized image in *Do Share Inspire* that has stopped Apple taking it, an issue I will be addressing shortly.

Regardless of the site you are publishing on, find their FAQs, download any of their formatting documents, and watch their videos – it may save you a lot of time and even money.

PRINT PRODUCTION

Following on from the previous section, we can assume that you've selected your POD vendor, and downloaded their file requirements. Those requirements should have been given to your designers, or followed by you (if you are doing any of this yourself).

Final spine width calculation

Once the interior design of the book is complete, you will know how many pages the book will be. Most of these services will offer some sort of calculation tool for you to work out the width of the spine – noting that the paper you choose will have an impact on width.

Go to your vendor site and calculate the spine width, then advise your cover designer. Some vendors will give you a template to download, so you will need to give that file to your designer. If you are using IngramSpark, you will not only have a template to download, but that template will already include the barcode for your book (yes, they produce this free of charge). Make sure you use their cover creator and send that PDF on to your designer, with the instructions for the required file type.

Create your title

Once you have the completed cover and interior files (likely to be PDF for most sites), create your title on their system, and upload the files. To create your title, you will need to include a range of details, which you should already have for the book. This will include details like:

- Title and subtitle.

- Names of author(s) and any other contributors.

- Number of pages.

- Dates of publication and release.

- Description of your book – you will probably need a short description too; the description is likely to include your back cover copy.

- Editorial or review quotes.

- Your chosen subject categories.

- Age range.

- Keywords.

You should be able to edit all of these details before the book is finalised and published into the world. These details are also the type of content you need for your ISBN registration, Kindle book and any other registrations you might need to complete (like your government's national library). I would recommend putting these details into a Word document once you have completed them here, so you have quick and easy reference to them for the other purposes – I've included a starter template for this in your downloads.

Once you have set up the title details, upload your cover and interior files and submit them into the vendor's process. This process will vary, depending on your vendor. With IngramSpark, the files go through an electronic validation to check that they satisfy the minimum requirements. After that, they go into a process where a person is involved in checking the files and creating a digital proof of your book. You will receive notification of that digital proof, and you are required to sign that off before you can order a physical proof – note, no one else can order the book until you enable it for distribution.

The other vendors should have similar processes, but they may vary slightly. Either way, once you have the ability to order a physical proof of your book do it; don't use the digital proof of a printed book to make the decision that it's good to go.

Review proofs and correct

This is where it starts to get very exciting, because you will be holding an actual copy of your book – like a real book! I cannot express how surreal this experience was for me, it's still a little strange to hold a copy of my book.

The concept of this proof copy is to check that nothing went wrong between the electronic files you submitted, and printing the book.

Check that the cover appears as you expected, particularly that the colours are correct; flick through the book and check that the images are all clear and as you expect them to be; check the footers and page numbers; check that the chapter headings are right, and the list goes on. It should not be a requirement to read this proof copy, you should have the copyediting and proofreading sorted by this point.

Once you have checked it all you need to do one of two things:

- If there are any issues that you do not believe were in your electronic files, go to the POD vendor and query the content/quality; work with them to resolve it.

- If it is as you expected, enable it for distribution – this means you are ready for post-production pre-launch activities.

EBOOK PRODUCTION

Like the print production, you should know who your ebook distributor will be by this stage. I'm going to outline this on the assumption you are using a different provider for ePub and Mobi; if you aren't, simply ignore the sections you don't require. If you have no idea what I mean by that, read on.

In the publishing world an ebook is something that has been designed and formatted to work with e-reading devices and software. There are two different type of ebook files:

- Mobi – this is the Kindle format for ebooks.

- ePub – the format used by everyone else (Kobo, iPad, Nook etc).

A PDF is not an ebook, in the sense we are discussing here. A PDF book is fixed in formatting and layout, and is more like your physical book in electronic format. An ebook is altogether different, where the reading device can alter the formatting and structure.

These files are largely produced as flowable ebooks, that is they are not designed to have pages or formatting like a real book. It is possible to create fixed layout ebooks, but not through the standard online conversion tools. If you want to create a fixed layout, I suggest engaging the services of an ebook developer.

Now this is a bonus if you are a writer and not that great in the visual sense, because if you are going to publish in the e-reader format then you do not have to be concerned about white space, fonts or generally making your book look pretty. However, if you want to design a 'book' in the traditional sense and you enjoy playing with layout and fonts, this format is likely to annoy you with its limitations.

You can still include colours and graphics in your ebook, but you have to be very careful how you apply these elements, since they can cause formatting issues. For example, many e-readers allow the reader to change the background from white to black, so it's easier to read in low light. If you've hard-coded your font to be black... well it might be limiting.

Selecting an ebook developer

If you believe that this task is beyond you, this is the point where you need to find an ebook developer. If you are using a POD vendor who offers a range of support services, you might find that they can perform this service for you – find out exactly what you get for the money, and what it will cost to make future changes if you do this.

If you are using a vendor who does not offer the service, ask around; or try some of the online services, like Fiverr. At this point I should probably say I have never used Fiverr, but I know quite a few people in the online communities I am part of who rave about the service they get from the Fiverr vendors.

Again, make sure you know exactly what you are getting from them, and whether you will have easy access to make future changes to your ebook files – particularly with the Mobi format.

Convert your front cover

The cover file you were given should be the entire wrapped cover (front, spine and back). For your ebook, you only need a front cover. If you thought ahead, you should have asked the cover designer to give you a JPG of your front cover for the ebook, in the required format and size outlined by your ebook vendor.

If you didn't get this, or if you designed your own front cover, you will need to convert that file to the appropriate format. Make note of the size requirements, file type, DPI/PPI and colour settings required by the vendor – ePub and Mobi aren't that different, but I think Mobi is stricter.

Have this file ready to go for upload when you create your title.

Convert interior to ePub

Do you remember that I mentioned you need to understand and follow all of the rules for your vendor? This is where that's going to bite you if you didn't. Some ePub vendors will do the conversion on their website; they want you to upload a Word document that meets their requirements. This sounds like an easier option, but there are some limitations with it – and you need to ensure you followed every rule, like not using tabs, removing headers and footers, and more.

My advice to ensure that this all runs smoothly, and to guarantee there isn't something weird in your Word document that will cause unintended consequences is:

- Copy your entire proofread document out of Word and onto Notepad.

- Start a fresh Word Document, following the formatting limitations outlined by your vendor.

- Paste all of the content back in.

- Apply the required styles and freshly insert your images.

The first time I created an ePub, it kept glitching because of something hidden in a heading that I couldn't see or remove. I ended up completely deleting the line and doing the heading again before it would go away. I also had glitches with an image in Mobi the first time around – Word hides a lot of code from you, so if there was a lot of editing of your manuscript, consider the steps above to start clean.

Note: change the ISBN from your physical book to the one for your ePub before converting it – unless you are including both ISBNs in your imprint.

If you are using a vendor's conversion tool, download the requirements and follow them, they'll tell you if it's right or wrong when you upload the file.

If you are required to submit an ePub, which I think is preferable because you ultimately have more control, then do I have the tool for you! It's called Calibre ebook management, and it's fantastic. Now, there are a range of other tools you can get, including online tools, to convert your Word or PDF document into an ePub, but I love Calibre – and not just because it's free.

Note: I do have qualms about the tool since it seems to remove Digital Rights Management and allow anyone to convert an ebook into any format – but as a self-publisher it's so easy to use.

The reason I enjoy it so much, is because it has a code editor that allows you to go in and play with the HTML for the ePub file. So, if it doesn't look like you had planned once it's been converted, then you can go in and fix it up. Now, I know this is not a function that everyone will enjoy, but I do not hide the fact I'm a bit of a tech-nerd. More importantly, it means that I now understand this much better, and I can make changes and improvements quite easily.

If you don't like the code, that's okay too. You have a range of options to select from for the conversion, and you can keep going back and forth by editing your Word document until you get it right – and you have more positive control over being able to change the file.

I'm not going to explain how to use this tool, they have a fantastic online manual for that.

Convert interior to Mobi

Again, go to Kindle and download the Kindle formatting guide, then follow the rules. You can upload a Word document, but Amazon recommends converting your file into HTML for the best results – this is where my next bit of advice fits in. I like to create my Mobi file from the ePub, and not just because I edit the ePub rather than the

Word document. When you converted to that format, decisions were made about the structure and format from Word to HTML; if you create your Mobi from the Word document, or Word generated HTML, some of the decisions might come out a little different.

Note: remove the ISBN from your Mobi, since Amazon issues an ASIN, which you do not need to include in the book.

Further to that reason, Calibre will do the ePub to Mobi conversion for you, so why wouldn't you use that functionality? Well, to be honest, I recently stopped using Calibre for the Mobi generation. Instead I went pure geek and downloaded KindleGen from Amazon, and I use this tool for the conversion – it is a command line tool that is quite simple to use, if you understand what I mean by a 'command line' tool.

Seriously though, if you don't want to play with the code – use Calibre to turn the Word document into an ePub, and then use it to turn the ePub into Mobi. As long as you do not have complex elements, and you did your formatting the right way, it should come out the way you wanted it to.

Proof the ePub and Mobi files

The only clunky thing about Calibre is the preview screen. It's alright, but I find it isn't as good as downloading a proper e-reader to proof the files. For the ePub files I tend to use Kobo, or put them on my phone and use iBooks. For Mobi, download the Kindle reader, or you can use Kindle Previewer to view the result for multiple Kindle devices.

Once you have converted your files, open them in the appropriate e-reader and perform the same sort of proofing checks as you did with the physical book. Again, it's not about reading the content, but making sure that the headings, content, quotes and images all appear the way you would expect them to appear. The content should be correct by now.

You might find that there are problems, in which case you can go back to the Word document, amend the formatting and do it all again. My recommendation is to get the ePub right before you convert and proof the Mobi; it saves time.

Note: if you need to make changes and go through the conversion and proofing again, delete the previous version of the ebook from your e-reader first.

Upload the files to your vendor

If you decide to use Amazon (CreateSpace/Kindle), you will need to find another vendor to do your ePub ebooks – the previous list has some good options. If you decide to use IngramSpark or BookBaby, then you can do it all in one place – actually, you will not need to convert your book into a Mobi format, since they will do that for you and publish it into KDP. So you only have to be worried about uploading the ePub and front cover to the publisher's website.

This is where I reiterate that I think you should seriously consider managing your own Kindle Store, and not use a third-party to publish your Kindle books onto Amazon. I say this for a number of reasons:

1. It's a relatively easy interface to use, and you will have complete control, with no additional costs.

2. Kindle revenue is one of the lowest in ebooks, and you don't need to share any of that with a third-party.

3. You can format the book description and editorial review to highlight particular content – the editorial review content comes through as one chunk from IngramSpark.

4. If you intend to do a KDP Select period, prior to the other ebooks coming out, you have to have your own account.

Either way you plan on doing it, once you have converted the front cover and interior, you can upload that content to your vendor's site. Depending on the site you're using, you might not have to recreate the title content – you might be able to add the electronic files into the physical book title you created earlier. If you need to create a new title, remember that Word document with all of the content, to make sure it's the same.

Stage Four – Preparing to Launch

You're book, ebook and marketing plans are ready to go, but there are a lot of other things you need to sort out before you can have a successful launch – and even with these there are no guarantees of success, I don't care what the 'experts' say!

Self-publishing is not just about writing a book and putting in on Amazon, hoping it will sell. You might get a little bit of traction, but with so many other self-publishers out there you need to work hard to get your book noticed. If you have ever worked in marketing, then you might be the exception to what I'm about to say – this is where it starts to get extremely difficult and uncomfortable for most writers.

This is also where I remind you again that this book is not about sequential steps, some of these tasks can be undertaken during Stage Three. Use the project overview download to get a better idea about how that works.

POST-PRODUCTION/PRE-LAUNCH

Below are a range of mainly administrative tasks that you can now undertake to ensure that everything is ready for you to launch the book. Having said that, there are a couple of tasks in here that require you to ask other people for their support, in a variety of ways.

Update your ISBN details

This depends on the country you are in. With some countries you need to provide the book details upfront to be issued with an ISBN; in countries where you purchase the ISBN directly from a service, you can wait until now to enter all of the required information.

Either way, before you make the book available to the world, you want to make sure that your ISBN details are up to date. Where you can manage this yourself, go in and enter all the required information. If you have to advise someone else, do that as soon as you finalise all the details.

Note: when you are creating your ISBN registration files on myidentifiers.com.au, you can duplicate a file and attach a different ISBN to it – this makes it simple to create a second record for your ebook, without starting from the beginning.

Finalise your author website pages

Your author website should be well established by now, with a sales page ready to go for the book. But it will be lacking a few essential elements that you need to finalise before you start promoting it:

- **Book cover** – remember way back in Designing the Cover I mentioned that you should get a mock-up of the book from your designer? Well even if you don't remember, you need to have a cover picture on your sales page, and it's preferable, although not essential, that looks like an actual book, not just a flat image.

- **Book preview** – when you buy a book from Amazon, you might have noticed they have a 'Look Inside' function where you can see the Table of Contents and pages from the first chapter. Consider creating your own PDF preview of your book, allowing people to get an idea of exactly what it is before they make a decision to buy it. This is something they can do in a bookshop; you need to replicate that experience to some degree online.

- **Sales video** – you have the sales copy, but people enjoy colour and movement as well; readers enjoy connecting with the author in different ways. Consider recording a simple three-minute sales video, introducing yourself and sharing something about the book; what you hope they get from the book; why you wrote the book; what the story means to you; or anything else along those lines. I would not recommend you spend money having a professional do this. If you (or a friend) have a decent smartphone and basic editing skills, you can create something honest and brief as another way of connecting with your potential audience.

- **Media kit** – add your media kit to your website, include a link from the sales page as well.

- **Gather testimonials and reviews** – make sure that any interesting and influential content is included in your sales page (see Reviews section for more).

- **Links to online stores** – once your book is available online, make sure you go back to the sales buttons or links you created earlier and send them through to the correct URL. This is where you can also earn yourself some extra money, over and above your royalty payments – use affiliate links where possible.

Affiliate sales links

I will start this section by saying that this won't work for everyone reading this book, but if you can use affiliate marketing links, do it.

Basically, many online stores have an affiliate program, where they pay you a small amount of money if someone buys the book through a link from your website – yes, it's that easy! Interestingly, it's not just for your own book either. When you join the affiliate program you can get links for any books, or other products sold by these stores. To make it even more interesting, it's not just the product you provided a link for – if someone clicks your book link, and buys other books, you get affiliate income for all of the products purchased during that session.

Amazon and Apple both have good affiliate programs – sign up and use these as the links for your own books, and for links to other products that you might share or recommend on your website.

Make sure that any links you put on your website or in social media are affiliate links; you are losing money for no good reason if you are sending people to Amazon, Apple or Barnes & Noble without using an affiliate link.

Note: all affiliate programs have rules, make sure you abide by them – for example, you cannot use affiliate links inside your Kindle ebooks.

Check online bookstores

Once you've made it available for distribution, check the title and description details on all of the websites as soon as possible. The last thing you want is to have incorrect information, and it can take a couple of days to get changes made back through your POD vendor.

Some POD vendors allow you to set the On Sale Date and Publication Date as different dates. This means you can get the book online and allow pre-sales to occur, but people are not yet able to get actual copies of the book. I find that this is a nice feature to allow you to get your book online, and get all of your links sorted, without feeling like you need to start promote the book just because it's live. It can give you a couple of days' grace, then you can start promoting the pre-sales.

It's also worthwhile to keep an eye on Goodreads, and claim your author page as soon as possible – I mentioned this in the marketing options. Same goes for your Amazon Author Spotlight if you haven't done this through Kindle already.

Organise your book launch

YOU DON'T HAVE TO LAUNCH AT A BOOKSHOP, YOU COULD HAVE IT AT A BAR, CAFÉ, LIBRARY, OR A VENUE THAT RELATES TO THE TOPIC OF YOUR BOOK

This might be an online celebration, or a local event where you gather people together to celebrate the launch of your book – but you should have some form of launch, and you need to start preparing for it now.

A launch is a great way to start generating buzz about your book, to get other people talking about it and sharing the fact that it's coming. There are many ways you can launch your book as well, and most of these require a fair amount of planning – which is what pre-launch is all about. Consider the following options:

- **Online launch with influencers** – are there bloggers or online personalities who align with your topic and might be interested in sharing your book with their audience? Reach out to them and see if they are interested in sharing the big launch day. It's important that you reach out with an offer for their audience, they want to know 'what's in it for me' to support you. Maybe you can give them a couple of free copies of the book; you could write a guest post on your topic with an angle for their audience; or maybe appear on their podcast. Reach out and ask, you truly never know.

- **Online launch with KDP Select** – if you are planning on publishing your ebook for the Kindle only, you can consider KDP Select 'free' or 'discount countdown' days. This is something you might also want to share with influencers – if they think it's valuable for their audience and they can give it to them for free, that's a win. Remember not to neglect the audience you already have with any of these promotions as well, they should know first and be prepared for it to happen.

- **Online launch and book tour** – online book tours were briefly discussed in the Marketing Options section. You can generate hype with a launch and book tour, again maybe align this to a KDP promotion, or offering some free copies for the tour hosts.

- **Local launch** – if you are publishing a physical book, then consider having a local launch for it. This could be at a bookshop, which requires you to find a local bookshop that is willing to stock your book and does book launches. It doesn't have to be at a bookshop though, you could have it at a bar, café, library, or a venue that relates to the topic of your book. For example, if you have written a novel with a museum as the main setting, you could have your launch in a museum. Or, if your non-fiction book is about wine appreciation, maybe a local vineyard.

A note on local book launches

As I'm writing this book, it's less than a week since my local book launch for *Do Share Inspire* – I had to wait a couple of months to lnch in the bookshop I wanted. Since this is still prominent in my memory, I thought I would include a couple of points to keep in mind – yep, some of them were learned the hard way.

- Create a running list of things you need to take with you on the night – everything you need, because your brain is unlikely to be functioning well.

- Plan your talk with enough time to practise it – by this I mean, try not to read it on the night. I don't do this anyway, I've gotten quite used to talking to rooms of people (the TEDx experience definitely kicked this up a notch for me); but you will be amazed how impressed people are if you can talk to them for 20 minutes without notes and umming. You are trying to impress them remember, so even if you can't do it for the entire talk, try to get some chunks where you don't need to read from paper. Remember, they are behind you and don't want to see you fail.

- Bring along two signup sheets for your newsletter, and keep one close to hand – I had two, but only one came out and I missed signing up three people that bought the book, because they had to hunt down the other sheet. It's a great time to get them interested in signing up for more from you. Promote it well and remember to take both signup sheets when you leave (yep, I left mine behind – luckily the bookshop was wonderful).

- If you can afford to cater, do it – the bookshop I used, Fullers, does a lot of launches, and has everything sorted out very well. I could have made alcohol available for people to buy their own; or I could have paid for the alcohol – I paid for the alcohol and we had cheese platters, which generated a nice atmosphere for the formalities. Sure, it chipped into the profits a little, but it's not like they had an open bar for three hours.

- Video it and have friends take photos – this is something you might use in future promotions, or to show other bookshops that you have the ability to engage a crowd with your book. The video does not need to be professional, it's not something you will share with everyone, and you might only take a couple of minutes out of it. This is a big deal, it's not every day you will launch a book, so gathering visual evidence of that will be worthwhile.

- Contact the media – you're going to be putting out press releases alongside the launch anyway, but contacting the local media with an invitation to attend could get you featured in the paper or local news. Reach out, and let them know why they should care about your book, highlighting any involvement you have in the community and local celebrities who might be involved.

- Plan nothing for the following day – this is not a note for everyone, but if you are even slightly introverted, and/or if you find the idea of this daunting, be prepared for the fallout. I felt physically shattered the day after my launch, and my brain was definitely not working anywhere near full capacity. A combination of massive amounts of adrenalin; introversion overload, as I ended up with about 100 people there, and many of course wanted to chat to me about the book; and a vulnerability hangover, as I did share some quite personal details in my talk. It really is a rollercoaster of emotions, so be kind to yourself in the celebration.

Finalise and commence your marketing plan

This document should be well underway by the pre-launch stage; you should already have started making contact with some influential people. It's important that you finalise this document now, because there are preparations that need to be undertaken, and you want to start the Launch stage knowing exactly what you need to do, and when.

As I mentioned in the section about developing the marketing strategy/plan, schedule in your milestones and review dates, so you can evaluate the success of your plan as you go along. You might find that you need to adjust it a few times; that options you thought would work, don't; options you had planned for haven't come off. This might mean you can reschedule items, or shift focus in activities.

REVIEWS AND TESTIMONIALS

This is where is starts getting tricky, because you haven't released your book to the world yet, but it is helpful for you to get at least a half dozen reviews early. Remember, earlier I mentioned you should not 'buy' reviews, and that can be through paying reviewers or a 'you review mine, I'll review yours' bartering system. So you have to use other ways to get them, and you have to allow some lead time for this to happen.

Below are some possible avenues for you to consider; I would recommend that you create a structured process of asking and prompting these people. It is far too easy for someone to forget to write their review, so I would recommend setting up a spreadsheet to capture when you sent them the book. Use this spreadsheet to schedule in reminders, one at an agreed time afterwards – maybe a week or two; one a couple of weeks after that; a last one reminding them that the book is launching soon and the value of their review to that launch.

Note: some of these can be done before you have printed copies of the book, through a PDF or ebook. If someone is influential, and you are not asking for a testimonial to include in the book itself, wait for printed copies.

Your audience

Do you already have a mailing list or social media audience? If so, go out to them and ask if anyone is interested in a preview copy of the ebook in exchange for a review – make it a select number so you aren't giving out copies to everyone.

Friends and colleagues

If your book is something you know particular friends or colleagues would be interested in, approach them with the offer of a free copy in exchange for a review (this might be a PDF version if you don't have the book published yet). Above all else, ask them for an honest review of the book.

Proofers

Ask your editor or anyone who helped proofread your book if they would be interested in writing a short review – they might not, but they might have found it interesting and/or valuable.

Work testimonials

For non-fiction books: is the book on a topic that is part of your career or day job? You can use testimonials or positive feedback from clients or respected colleagues, about your skill in the topic.

Influencers and leaders

Again, non-fiction: do you know any leaders in the field you're writing about who you could approach with an advanced review copy of the book? These might be the influencers I mentioned in the book launch section, prominent business people in the community, leaders of government or industry, media influencers, or university academics.

You might be surprised who is willing to help if you, start asking around. You should definitely consider approaching anyone who helped with the book, if you interviewed people or had to ask them for a release on their material as part of your copyright process. People enjoy promoting something if they were part of the process of creating it. Note: if possible, offer these people a physical copy of the book.

A review service

Review services are not considered 'buying' reviews. There are a number of online services you can submit your book to, and they will make the ebook available to their audience for review. Yes, you do pay them for the service of hosting and sharing your book with their audience, but the reviewers themselves are not paid in any way. Story Cartel is one such service, but there are many others.

Review blogs

Do a web search for people who do review blogs – there are hundreds of them out there. You will require a longer lead time for some of these reviewers, so you cannot be guaranteed of a particular date. Read their requirements, since many online reviewers do not accept self-published titles.

Traditional media

As a self-publisher, it's more difficult to get your foot in the door with magazines and newspapers, but I'm assured it isn't impossible. Chances are you are not going to break that market with your first self-published book, but you never know unless you try.

GETTING IN BOOKSHOPS

If you are planning on publishing a physical book, you are likely to want to see your book in bookshops – it's a very surreal experience. While you could try to use a distributor, given the per unit price of POD books, it means you would end up with less than 50c per book sold. Now, I know I mentioned that you were unlikely to get rich from publishing, but you should be aiming for a better profit margin than that – and the fact is that a distributor will not sell your book better than you can yourself.

I haven't sorted out how to do this well for myself yet, but I will share with you what I do know, and what I have found in my research – hopefully this is a section of the book I can add more to as I continue through the physical self-publishing journey.

Contact the bookshops you want

You might remember that I said you should read a lot if you want to write, it helps you develop and learn the craft. It follows then, that I believe you should love books – and if you love books you should have a favourite bookshop. Okay, I'll concede you may not need to love bookshops, but why would you not?

I've travelled to every Australian state and territory; I've even lived in four of them. So, when I started thinking about bookshops I would like my book to be in, there was a list of about a dozen stores I knew I wanted to approach. As well as the ones I loved, I went online and searched for popular independent bookshops throughout the country.

With a list of 20 bookshops, I then sought their contact details – phone numbers and emails, preferably of the manager. The goal was to go out to each of these bookshops, starting with an email that introduced me and my book, and asking them if they would be interested in stocking it. If you're in Australia, this process becomes a lot easier using the Find a Bookshop option on the Australian Booksellers website booksellers.org.au. So far, I have made contact with 30 bookshops throughout the country, and four are currently stocking copies.

Let's take a step back. My first step was to approach a local bookshop, because I wanted to make sure the book was stocked in my home town. Fortunately, there is a bookshop I love in Tasmania, and it was also the bookshop I wanted to have my launch in. Even more fortuitous for me was the fact that the year prior I had approached them to stock a couple of gift products I created, so I already had a slight relationship with the Manager and I wasn't going in cold.

After they accepted the book, I tried for the next bookshop I desperately wanted to get into in Victoria. I reached out and was given the contact details for the person who manages consignment books; I haven't had any luck with email, so I think I'm going to have to call them. Then I tried a bookshop in the north of Tasmania, another one with a fantastic atmosphere. This one I decided to approach in person, because I think that it does work better that way. They agreed to take 10 copies of the book on consignment.

What I'm discovering is that people respond better to the in-person contact, and that can be a phone call. Two other bookshops, one in Wollongong and the other in Melbourne, have taken consignment copies after a phone conversation. This will be limiting if I start trying to push the book in overseas stores, but I've adjusted to a combined approach for Australia. Send an email first, trying to entice them with what the book is about; offering them an ebook preview if they want to know more. From there I discuss that I am a self-published author and how they can purchase the book from either myself or IngramSpark's distribution network; with a few of them I also discuss the possibility of a book signing event. A week after the email, if I haven't heard back, I should call them to discuss the book.

I say 'should' because this is far more difficult than you might expect. It is tricky trying to disengage your emotions and sense of worth from this process, which makes these calls very challenging. The result is that I procrastinate, and find almost anything to do other than making these phone calls. Hopefully, you are better at this than I am.

What is on consignment?

Book purchasing contains an element of risk, since there is always the possibility that for some reason the book won't sell very well. For this reason, many bookshops reduce their risk by taking books from small publishers and self-publishers on consignment only, or purchasing from a wholesaler who has a returns policy.

What does on consignment mean? Well it means that you give them the books and they don't pay you unless the books sell. If they sell, you get paid and they might even re-order from you. If they partially sell, you get paid for the ones that sold and you take back the ones that didn't; they usually have a timeframe. If they don't sell at all, you just take them back.

Now, if you include postage, and the fact that you get around 55% of the retail sale price, there is a chance that you can lose money on this – hey, I told you that if you're in this to make money you might be disappointed. It's something to think about when you are making decisions on who to approach.

This is also why picking the right POD vendor can come in handy – because some of them will allow the bookshops to return books for a refund, if they buy them directly; IngramSpark does this in a few countries. This makes it more appealing to the bookshops, and means you don't have to play middle man. The shops still have to outlay money up front for the books, but the risk is removed since they can return any unsold items for a refund. It's not essential, but it is something to be aware of about how bookshops work.

Using a POD vendor for this has another bonus. If a bookshop says yes, you can order the books directly from the POD vendor and have them shipped straight to the store. This removes some of the postal charge losses, and the books are well packaged to arrive without any damage. Another benefit of not having to ship books yourself.

Stage Five – Getting it Out There

We're at the launch point, your book is about to go live. You've spent the last couple of months getting it ready, and making sure that all of the marketing and PR is also ready to go. This is where you need to make sure all of your planning is done, because this is where all of the emotion will kick in – and you do not want to be making decisions during that emotion.

Your marketing plan should be set; everything and everyone should be ready to go. I had a spreadsheet of tasks that was down to the minute details of 'Email *person x*', 'Send press release to list', 'Create a launch image for my blog' – but it was also missing a lot of other detail that I wasn't prepared for. You want everything on a list, or else you will forget it. Oh, and if you have people helping you with the launch, then you want to make sure they have a list and are reporting in.

There is another point I want to make, before we get into the nitty gritty here: while we would all like to have great launches that get our books to the top of bestseller lists, you should not be thinking of this as a short game. We'll get into this at the end of this chapter, but you should consider the launch as merely the beginning of a one- to two-year commitment to your book (depending on your goals).

YOUR LAUNCH TEAM

SELF-PUBLISHING IS A ROLLERCOASTER OF EMOTIONS, YOU NEED PEOPLE AROUND TO REMIND YOU THAT IT'S NOT ALL CRAP, AND IT'LL BE OKAY

As a self-publisher, you might be doing this completely on your own – just you, beavering away at a keyboard, trying to get traction. This is largely how I've done it. While people in my community have shared the book and posts about the experience, there is a lot of this that is entirely solitary. What I've discovered is that the solitary nature of this can be quite difficult at times. With that in mind, I would recommend you consider including the following people in your team.

The cheerleaders

You might be a very confident person; completely certain that your book is brilliant and never entertaining any doubts about its quality or content – but I know that is highly unlikely. Even the most confident person would suffer through the angst of a book launch, I am certain of that!

For me, and I know I'm not alone, the rollercoaster is constant. I fluctuate between so many thoughts and emotions – ranging from a certainty that the book is crap and nobody should ever read it, through to confidence in what I'm doing and the story I'm telling; and every incarnation between. Just yesterday I woke up convinced that I should pull the book from publication, and shut down the website while I'm at it. Now, most of the time I'm simply focused on doing the tasks on my list, and I'm genuinely excited about people reading the book – but the outlier thoughts and emotions can throw an entire day into disarray.

All of this sharing is to raise the point that you need a support network; you need a couple of people who can talk you down from the ledge. These should be people who already understand your inherent craziness; people who have read your book; and people you trust to be honest with you. You don't need them to share your book, or take on any other roles in launching it – but you need them to be around to remind you that it's not all crap, and it'll be okay.

In my opinion, these people are the most important part of your launch team – everything else you can largely look after yourself in some way. I think that we often need other people's kindness and truth to destroy our own inner doubts and fears. You might feel you don't need it; great!

The arse kickers

Sometimes you will procrastinate over tasks that are a little too scary, or that you aren't entirely sure how to tackle – like phoning bookshops.

This is when you need the people/person who will keep you accountable for your actions – the people/person who will kick your arse until you do the tasks you set yourself.

There are a few options for the members of this team – friends; family; hire an accountability coach; join a writing group and get them to hold you accountable. The two most important traits are that they will nag you until you complete the tasks you need to finish; and they are willing to talk to you about the possible reasons why you aren't doing things. If it was just for reminders, you could put your project plan into a calendar; this is so much more.

I recommend having at least two, and they should have a copy of your project plan as well. Two means that if life gets in the way for one person, there is still a good chance that the other one is free to keep nagging – life will inevitably get in the way if you have no contingency, Murphy's Law.

The influencers

These are the people who have agreed to promote your book in some way. They might be sharing it with their audiences, writing a review for Amazon, featuring you on a blog, interviewing you on a podcast, or performing other promotional tasks. We've largely talked about them already in other sections, but I will mention here that you need to make their life as simple as possible. Provide them with details about the promotional activities, give them everything they need to easily promote you in the agreed way, and send appropriate reminders.

Also, remember to thank these people for any and all support they provide. People like being included in this sort of activity, and they like to be acknowledged for those contributions. You might even consider putting all of these people into a mailing list in MailChimp (or whatever subscriber service you use) so you can update them on the progress, and give shout outs to particular people. This can help them become even more engaged in the launch; just don't overdo it.

PRESS RELEASES

Hopefully, you have engaged a professional to create a press release for you – there is an art to knowing how to write to intrigue journalists; this is worthwhile paying for. If you have also engaged a PR company to release those details, then you can just sit back and let it happen.

If you are taking it upon yourself to send out the press releases, then you need to start this process a couple of weeks prior to the launch. This will give interested journalists time to consider the release and get in touch with you.

I mentioned earlier about the PR websites that you can use to distribute your press release. There are many free and paid options, but the most important element in using any of these sites is a good press release to start with.

Another point for this: journalists receive a tonne of press releases a day, so if you are exceptionally keen to get your story picked up by a particular journalist or site, try calling them as a follow up. Don't assume they saw your release and weren't interested; it simply might not have made it through the noise.

PODCASTERS AND BLOGGERS

If you are thinking that you want to use online sources like podcasts and blogs to promote your book, then you probably want an even longer lead time – unless you are happy for them to talk to you or feature you after the launch. Popular blogs and podcasts may be scheduled three months in advance, so if you want the story to align with the launch, plan ahead.

Yes, that means this content could be moved back into Stage Four, but I think it is more relevant in Stage Five since this is something you will continue to do long after the pre-launch process has completed. Remember, this is not a set of sequential steps.

Personally, I only reached out to a couple of sites for *Do Share Inspire*, because I gave myself a ridiculous timeframe to publish. Even if that wasn't the case, I wasn't too worried about creating a lot of hype and buzz at launch time – I'm playing the longer game, and trying to ensure that the story is drip fed out through various sources over a longer period of time.

Finding blogs

Hopefully, you are already familiar with blogs on your topic or sites that your audience reads. If you aren't familiar with the big players in your topic area, then how did you do your research about whether there is a market or need for your book? If you know a couple of sites, there are sources that will help you find others. One I prefer is SimilarWeb, (similarweb.com), which allows you to enter a URL, and it provides you with a range of details including traffic, referrals, and audience. Importantly, it also has a section on Similar Sites, which may help you discover like websites.

There are also a range of aggregation sites for blogs, sites that contain lists by topic/popularity/country etc. Just search Google for the 'top lifestyle blogs' or 'best Australian business blogs' and you are bound to find some of these sites. I like blogrank (blogmetrics.org) and I also like Blog Chicks in Australia (blogchicks.com.au).

It is extremely important that you read through the blog, the About pages, and any rules about contacting or submitting content to them before you pitch. You want to make sure that your book topic aligns to their content and audience, that they accept submissions or ideas from others, and that you provide them with all of the required information if they do. We'll talk about getting in touch with these influencers in a moment.

Finding podcasts

I've had an interesting history with podcasts. I used to listen to a couple a few years ago, but then I seemed to forget that they existed. During the time I forgot about them, podcasts really took off; for the last year I've gone back to them in a big way. In some ways, podcasting is the new blogging, and a lot of people have started podcasts in the last two years – a lot have also stopped podcasting in that time.

If you aren't a podcast listener already, then you are about to engage with the medium. It's a great way to get your message to a wider audience, and it moves entirely outside mainstream media. Remember how I said a lot of mainstream press won't review self-published books? Podcasts have no qualms about it; podcasting is pretty much 'self-published radio' after all!

The best place to start is iTunes; Apple has more podcasts than any other source, and some of their search functions are great for this. Below are some search ideas to find podcasts:

- Search by subject – if you're writing a business book then go as broad as business or as narrow as specific topics.

- Search by a famous person in your topic area – I searched for a variety of TED speakers when for *Do Share Inspire*.

- Search for a known podcast – if you have a favourite.

Once you have found some relevant podcasts, you can find a list of 'Listeners also subscribed to' at the bottom of the podcast's listing page; which might take you in a different direction.

Again, like the blogs, you need to listen to a couple of the podcasts to make sure you are familiar with the tone and structure. Most podcasts will have a website link on their listing page; visit that website to find out the process for contacting them about being a guest.

Contacting bloggers and podcasters

There are a number of free posts and content that will share details about submitting a guest post, asking for a blog review, and contacting podcasters – search on Google for more detail on this. My basic advice and rules are:

- Follow their rules! If they tell you how to contact them, and what they need from you, please give it to them.

- Know their content – even if you're new to the site or podcast, take the time to read some posts or listen to a couple of podcasts. How can you expect to tell them how you will provide value to their audience if you have no idea what they currently share with their audience?

- Make the pitch short, interesting and respectful – don't make them go somewhere else to find out the basics about you, this should all be in the pitch. You need to include: who you are, what you do, and why their audience would be interested in listening to you. This should only take a couple of sentences – remember it is a pitch.

- Follow up – give them about a week before you follow up with another email. Remember that everyone gets very busy, and sometimes things happen that distract them from that interesting email you sent through. If you don't get a response after the second one, you could try again in three to four weeks, just in case something very distracting did occur in their lives. If you still haven't had a response, well any other contact starts to become stalking.

- Be respectful – some podcasts and blogs are designed to have other people contributing, and the people that run these sites need people to talk to, or to submit content for them. Chances are, if you are reaching out about your new book, you need them far more than they need you! That doesn't mean you should grovel or ask from a place of desperation – but you should always acknowledge that it's their show/site; you would be grateful and help promote it; and if they choose not to have you, well that's fine too. Oh, and they do not owe you an explanation, or even an answer when it comes to that.

I recently watched a webinar from Nick Stephenson about working with podcasters, and he recommended that if someone comes back with a 'thanks but I don't think you've right for my audience', you should go back and ask them if they know any other podcasters who you might be a good fit for. People like to be asked for their expertise, and this might raise an option you hadn't considered. He also recommends asking podcasters this question a couple of weeks after you have appeared on their show – something to think about.

LAUNCH ANNOUNCEMENT ON YOUR SITES

You should also have a couple of great launch announcement graphics to share on social media, and to include on your author website. Get creative with these images, and ask people in your community to share the launch posts with their own communities.

If you have a blog, make sure you include a post about the experience of the launch – including your emotions and how excited you are that it's finally here. Your audience wants to go on this journey with you, they need to feel like they're sharing in the highs and the lows; okay, maybe not as much of the lows, that depends on who you are and what you write about.

PLAN AND PLAY THE LONG GAME

I mentioned earlier that the launch of your book shouldn't be considered a 'short-term' activity. Yes, it's great to have a lot of hype and promotion for the first couple of weeks, particularly if getting a good sales ranking is one of your goals. But it is more likely that you're going to have to work over a much longer timeframe to get the publicity and sales that you are looking for.

It's worthwhile to break this into various stages though, where your initial marketing plan covers the launch and first three months of promotion. Just prior to the end of this plan, you should examine what has been working, and what area you might need to spend more time focusing on – probably for about the next six months. The final marketing plan would cover the remainder of the year, and potentially a second year, depending on your goals for the book.

It's important to stick to your plan and not make knee-jerk changes based on other people's bright and shiny ideas. I cannot stress how emotional a book launch can be, and you need to be prepared for a range of emotions that you might not have expected. You also need to be prepared for the fact that everything is not going to work the exact way you thought it would – some promotional ideas will fall flat; others may work better than you expected. This is why you create a plan, because you need to trust the decisions that you made with a more rational mindset, and give it a chance to work.

That doesn't mean that you shouldn't consider new ideas that come up during your launch or further promotional period – but you need to analyse whether this new idea would align with your marketing strategy, and whether it will complement the activities you have already planned.

Playing the long game means that you are focused on the book for a longer period of time, making it a key part of your business, or your creative life. It also means you can reinvigorate book sales and promotion at key points – maybe giving copies away for your birthday, or the publishing anniversary. It also gives you a much greater chance of getting traction as an 'expert', if your book is non-fiction.

Just look at famous authors, and you can see that they live and breathe their books for a number of years after they're published. This is particularly true of non-fiction authors; remembering that the book might have taken years to research and write in the first instance, this makes complete sense.

Wrapping it Up

IT IS VERY EASY TO GET OVERWHELMED WITH THE AMOUNT OF INFORMATION THAT IS AVAILABLE ON ANY TOPIC NOWADAYS — STOP LOOKING FOR MORE

I hope you now have the confidence to take on this challenge. I've been as honest as I can about some of the more complex and difficult aspects of self-publishing – while providing you with step-by-step instructions and advice, that I wish I'd had before I self-published the first time.

Please remember to download the resources from the website – dinkylune.com/wtlstuff – you'll need the password (**Sc@recr0w**).

Personally, I think the empowerment we have all been given from the ability to self-publish our books is incredible. It is still my dream to be traditionally published; there is a validation in that process I would love to have, and it would be nice to have someone else looking after a many of the administrative and marketing elements for me. In the meantime, I still get to share my knowledge and advice with you in a very real and meaningful way. This is particularly important for topics that might not have the marketability required by publishing houses.

I know it can seem daunting to tackle self-publishing, although I truly believe the most difficult aspect is believing in yourself enough to do it. While there are many steps to turn your idea into a book and get it out into the world, following a checklist is the easy part. It takes a lot of courage to say 'this is good enough to share with the world', and that is what we're talking about here. If you start this thinking you will make a perfect book, it will never get done – nothing is ever perfect.

So, what are you waiting for? You know what you have to do – now it's simply up to you to have to courage to do it. I'd love to know when you do – feel free to email me, **kylie@dinkylune.com** to let me know when you publish.

REFERENCES AND RESOURCES

As I've mentioned, there are so many sources over the years that helped me acquire some of this knowledge; there is a lot that came from my own experience too. I've decided to capture the most influential sources here, ones I know contributed to these ideas in real and meaningful ways. While I have inevitably read other blogs or listened to other webinars, the sources below were the people who first shared ideas with me, and who I keep going back to for advice – they are the voices that inspire and help me.

It's interesting that as I gather this list together it occurs to me that I probably don't need to write this book, since there are so many experts who have written something similar. Then it occurs to me that is a limiting thought, because this book is an aggregation of all of their brilliance, and the lessons I learned the hard way.

- James Altucher – subscribe to his email list from his website; so many great ideas and wonderful vulnerability to keep you going when things turn to crap.

- Chandler Bolt – I have to spend more time with his material, but he has some interesting ideas, while reinforcing other voices.

- Book Riot The Podcast – this is one of the podcasts I discovered about five months ago, and I've consumed a fair amount of content since. It is more about industry news, which is great.

- Chris Brogan – I have learned a lot about online business and building an audience from Chris' books and blogs over the years. This helped with some of the marketing and launch ideas.

- Ray Edwards – I've recently completed a couple of basic copywriting courses from Ray. His PASTOR method for writing sales copy has been particularly useful.

- Seth Godin (Skillshare and Udemy courses) – I've probably learned more about identifying and connecting and strategising from Seth than anyone else. And he helps us all see what is possible when you decide to publish for yourself

- Jeff Goins – another email to subscribe to. I will admit that I haven't read his *Art of Work* book, but the community seems to think it's great.

- Tim Grahl (Your First 1000 Copies and recent webinars) – I've only recently been introduced to Tim's content, he has some interesting insights and simple tips.

- Kristen Joy (The Book Ninja) – great course that gave me quite a few tips, including introducing me to IngramSpark.

- Guy Kawasaki and Shawn Welch, *APE: Author, Publisher, Entrepreneur: How to Publish a Book*, Nononina Press USA, 2013. This is the first book I read on the topic of self-publishing. I had read many blog posts before this, but I think there is a lot of underlying knowledge I have about it that came from this book.

- Laura Pepper Wu (Skillshare book launch course) – her course helped in my first self-publishing journey, and I wished I'd reviewed it before launching *Do Share Inspire*.

- Ramit Sethi (I Will Teach… and Zero to Launch) – this is all about creating and launching courses, but the best crossover material was writing sales pages.

- Dana Sitar – I learned a lot about being brave with my writing, and the self-publishing space from Dana's content.

- Nick Stephenson (First 10K Readers) – only recently introduced to him, and I loved his webinars and book. His advice on connecting with podcasters has had a huge influence.

- Thomas Umstattd Jr & James L Rubart (The Novel Marketing Podcast) – heaps of marketing ideas and tips, presented in a very approachable way. I already had a well-developed platform and brand, but I think that material is great too.

- Kathy Ver Eecke (getabookdeal101.com) – her course taught me how to pitch a book to a traditional publisher. Might sound weird for self-publishing, but some of those skills and knowledge have been important for other tasks in talking about my book.

I have included links to all of these materials, and a few other blogs that I think you should consider reading through, on the resource page. Don't forget to visit and download resources dinkylune.com/wtlstuff – password is **Sc@recr0w**.

A CAUTIONARY NOTE

It is very easy to get overwhelmed with the amount of information that is available on any topic nowadays, and self-publishing is one of the big ones. You could spend a whole year consuming books, courses, podcasts, webinars and blogs on the topic; and I'm sure that many people have done just that.

When I started my own business I went through this 'learning' process – I didn't know what I didn't know, so I consumed everything I could. Sometimes this was to fill the gaps in my knowledge, but often I continued to look for sources because I was scared of 'doing'; or I thought someone would give me the silver bullet that would make it 'easy'. Talking with other people on the same journey as me, I know I am not alone in these thoughts, feelings and actions.

I've lost more time than I care to think about in the last two years, and I've created more anxiety for myself in the process. If you've gotten this far, you have all the basic knowledge to start self-publishing; seriously, you do. You have more knowledge than I did when I self-published my books – yes, even more than when I published *Do Share Inspire* just last year.

So, while I've provided additional resources, you don't need them! They aren't going to give you anything that makes this process 'easy'; self-publishing requires you to get stuck in and do the work. Please feel free to go to any and all of these resources for additional detail and information, they are all great. But, do not delay your leap into self-publishing to consume their content – start with what you have now, or you will likely never start.

Are you ready to start? Are you brave enough to try? I know it's scary, but I also know that you can do it.

Want More from Kylie?

If you enjoyed this book, and you're interested in getting more content from Kylie, there are a couple of options for you.

BUY A COPY OF *DO SHARE INSPIRE*

If you've ever felt frustrated with where you are; if you feel like you aren't living the life you want; if you are tired of consuming inspiration and not doing anything with it – experience the life-changing adventure of My Year of TED. Visit kyliedunn.com/doshareinspire for more.

SIGN UP FOR FREE CONTENT

Kylie has two mailing lists that you can join, for free:

- kyliedunn.com/signup – you'll get *Finding Your Way Home, Living an Aligned Life, Less Stress – More Happiness* and more.

- dinkylune.com/signup – you'll get *Tools, Themes & Plugins I Use, Strategic Plan on a Page* and other Guides for Writers and Bloggers.

Acknowledgements

I've made note of the wonderful people whose ideas have helped me gain much of the knowledge needed to venture into self-publishing – but knowledge and ideas are only part of the challenge. There are a number of other people in my life who have given me the courage to self-publish; to believe that what I have to say should be more broadly shared; and the confidence that people will find it interesting and insightful.

Thank you to all of my supportive and friends and family, your praise and encouragement through the *Do Share Inspire* experience has been invaluable to my sanity and confidence that I can do this. Particularly everyone who was involved in my not-a-book-launch and official book launch; your support at these events was invaluable.

Thank you also to Joy, for the brilliant feedback on the draft version of this book, it helped me see some of the small gaps that I needed to fill. Also, to Merridy, for the wonderful job editing and supporting me with this book.

To the new friends I've made through publishing *Do Share Inspire*, and the professionals in the book industry who have provided me with insights to do it better in the future.

Lastly, thank you Derek, for providing such a wonderfully supportive environment that allows me to continue to pursue this crazy dream of mine – hopefully it will pay off one day.

About the Author

Born in Wollongong, NSW, the middle child of a working class family, Kylie always thought that she didn't know what she wanted to be when she grew up – but if you'd asked young Kylie she would have told you that she wanted to be an author, to write books that inspire other people.

Kylie is the self-published author of *Do Share Inspire: The Year I Changed My Life Through TED Talks*, and some much smaller ebooks. She published her first ebook in 2013, and has been on a steep learning curve about the self-publishing world ever since.

Since changing her life through TED Talks in 2011-12, Kylie has continued to push outside her comfort zone, and tackle new experiences; aerial circus being one of her newfound passions. Now an author, TEDx speaker, trainer and consultant, Kylie focuses on trying to explain the world to people – in a way that helps them build the knowledge and skills to live better lives.

She does this with the loving support of her partner Derek and their beloved crazy dog Lily; from the comfort of the house they built together in Tasmania's Huon Valley.

www.ingramcontent.com/pod-product-compliance
Lightning Source LLC
Chambersburg PA
CBHW072148020426
42334CB00018B/1923